Defying Decrepitude:
A Personal Memoir

Defying Decrepitude:
A Personal Memoir

Alan Peacock

With an introduction by Lord Sutherland
Illustrations by Elizabeth Le Drew

Not many know how to be old.

Duc de La Rochefoucauld
Maxims, 1678

Published by
The University of Buckingham Press

Copyright © Alan Peacock 2013.

The moral rights of the author have been asserted. No part of this publication may be reproduced, stored in a retrieval system or transmitted in any form or by any means without the prior permission in writing of the author.

Every reasonable effort has been made by the author to trace and acknowledge the copyright holders of any third-party material in this book. Any errors or omissions should be notified in writing to the author.

Illustrations by Elizabeth-Alice Le Drew.

ISBN 978 1 908684 25 7

Printed and bound in Great Britain by
Marston Book Services Ltd, Didcot, Oxon

The author

Sir Alan Peacock is one of the better known British economists of recent times. He has combined an academic career with activist engagement in policy, and is probably best known for *The Peacock Report on the Financing of the BBC* (1986). He has been successively a wartime sailor (1942–45); reader in public finance at the London School of Economics (1951–56); professor of economics in four major universities (1957 to date); a senior civil servant as chief economic adviser to the Department of Trade and Industry (1973–76); principal and then vice chancellor (president) of Britain's only independent university, Buckingham (1979–85); and consultant and adviser to a wide range of international agencies, governments and professional bodies. Now a professor emeritus, he is an honorary professor in public finance at Edinburgh Business School, Heriot-Watt University.

His contributions to economics and to public affairs have been recognised by eleven honorary degrees, fellowships of the British Academy, the Royal Society of Edinburgh (RSE) and the Italian National Academy. He was awarded the Royal Medal of the

RSE in 2002, having previously been knighted for public service in 1987.

Other books with an autobiographical flavour by Alan Peacock

Paying the Piper: Culture, Music and Money (Edinburgh University Press, 1993)
The Enigmatic Sailor (Whittles Publishing, 2003)
Anxious to Do Good: Learning to Be an Economist the Hard Way (Imprint Academic, 2010)

Acknowledgments

It will be clear from Chapter 1 that I am deeply indebted to Dr Colin Currie FRCPE for offering the stimulus that resulted in this work.

I am grateful for the comments and criticisms voiced by readers of an earlier manuscript, which have resulted in what I hope are improvements to the text. These included such 'prominente' as Tony Culyer, Alan Maynard and Nicholas Bosanquet, erstwhile colleagues at York and well known experts in the economics of medicine.

On the production side, I was lucky to have the assistance of two colleagues at Edinburgh Business School. Stuart Allan has applied his editorial expertise in pointing out infelicities of style that I have endeavoured to correct. Connie Paton shouldered the task of processing several drafts of the work, doing so with the patience of a saint.

The career of Lord Sutherland embodies so many facets of public life requiring deep understanding and expertise of the human condition that his willingness to introduce this work – suitably warning the reader of its 'quirkiness'! – is a rare privilege for reader and author.

I would also like to thank Elizabeth Le Drew who created the front cover and the cartoons.

***

The Maxims of Francois, Duc de La Rochefoucauld appeared in 1665. I acknowledge my debt to their translator, Leonard Tancock, whose work can be found in the Penguin Classics edition of La Rochefoucauld, first published in 1959.

.

Contents

Introduction by Lord Sutherland of Houndwood — i

Chapter 1: Your life to come — 1
The costs and benefits of lengthening the lifespan

Chapter 2: Living beyond one's allotted span — 7
The scene is set by the visit of a seventy (plus)-year-old to a medical practice

Chapter 3: The perils of preservation — 17
uncovered. Coming to terms with 'healthspeak' in recommended clinical appointments

Chapter 4: The questionnaire disease — 27
'There has to be change for things to remain the same': inmates ask the same questions and the answers are often distressingly familiar; the mixed legacy of Florence Nightingale

Chapter 5: Journey's beginning — 39
Decrepitude and plans for retirement

Chapter 6: The dark shadow of decrepitude — 51
Facing the fact that the 'old engine' (the human

body) needs a series of major repairs as well as fine-tuning

Chapter 7: How was it in your day, Dad?   73
The recognition that the old help to satisfy the intense curiosity in the past of the young

Chapter 8: 'The strife is o'er ... the battle lost'   95
The travails of loss of physical independence; how the old may and do help the aged

Chapter 9: Defiance gives way to resignation   107
Decrepitude and bereavement

Epilogue: The changing relationship between doctor and patient   115

Endnotes   119

Introduction

Defying Decrepitude is like a rich multi-coloured tapestry: a bright thread here, a darker strain there. Our eyes are directed by tensions of reds yellows and blues, while our minds find illumination in unexpected juxtapositions of detail and generality.

It leads us gently and at times quirkily through the process identified in the title via the later life and memories of one of our most distinguished economists. Alan Peacock tells it as he has lived it, with a mixture of objectivity, humour, and the particularity that old age gives us.

Occasionally a memory illuminates a present reality, and the schoolboy prefigures the future economics professor and guru. (Interestingly, the rules of playground engagement and classroom warfare in the Dundee of the late 1920s and early 1930s do not seem very different from those of my post-war primary school in Aberdeen.)

The outwardly conforming hospital and dental patient – mischievous in thought always, in words sometimes – is a reassurance to us all that there are routes of sanity and survival through increasing confrontation between man and bureaucracy. Where credit is due, where the bureaucracy reveals its ultimately benign intentions, credit is given and ways of survival are charted via the distinctiveness of Alan Peacock's words and mind.

This is a unique and, I use the word again, 'quirky' autobiographical encouragement to the rest of us engaged in, or about to be engaged in, defying decrepitude. Read on...

Stewart Sutherland KT, FRSE, FBA, FKC
Lord Sutherland of Houndwood KT, FBA

1. Your life to come

The origin of this work is several conversations with Dr Colin Currie FRCPE, eminent specialist in geriatric medicine and author of two absorbing novels on the passage from medical student to consultant. I met him by chance on the train from Edinburgh Waverley to King's Cross. He was advising the then prime minister, Gordon Brown, on the future of medical services for the aged. As a result I considered that the NHS, whatever government was in power, should know more about 'client' encounters with its services and wrote a pamphlet entitled 'Growing Old Disgracefully'. Encouraged by Dr Currie's reaction to it and that of fellow oldies, I decided to expand it into a book. In the course of examining my own experiences more closely, I discovered that the process of ageing has a profound effect on the relationship between doctor, specialist and patient – even more so if the patient's lifespan becomes longer. The result is a rather different book from the one that I had intended to write.

The prevailing ethos of the medical profession requires that improvements in their knowledge should abound to the welfare of the old through

DEFYING DECREPITUDE: A PERSONAL MEMOIR

keeping them alive longer. Led on by the succession of headlines in our dailies, this offers good news to counteract the miseries of the world of which we are only too well aware as the result of the modern marvels of instant reportage. I share the wonderment of those who observe the skill, persistence and dedication that pervades the medical laboratories. I have seen my own expectation of life at 60 rise progressively. I cannot have reached nonagenarian status at the same time as all my three children have reached pensionable age without having benefited from the results of scientific progress in medicine.

The allocation of more resources to medical research means that the community must be prepared to pay higher taxes and/or offer larger donations to medical charities. This is widely – perhaps even cheerfully – accepted, although controversy about how this money is allocated between different lines of research and how costs are to be controlled remain. What is less obvious is that the progressive increase in the medical input to achieve this end requires closer cooperation from the client in the form of attendance at clinics, which often leads to both continuous treatment and much more time spent under medical surveillance and care. In other words, the benefits of living longer have to be matched against their 'cost', notably the extra time and energy required of the client in attending surgeries or clinics for advice and treatment. The changing pattern of treatment through time may add the further necessity of greater participation by the client, aided or unaided by helpers, in its prosecution.

As an economist I shall be expected to construct some kind of prognosis of the nature and magnitude of this change in the balance between the input of medical services, including the time input of patients, and the output of benefits (mainly the extra years of life), allowing for how much future time will be taken up by 'repair and maintenance' to the human machine. One might sniff out some interesting relationship between the inputs and outputs, perhaps a version of the law of diminishing returns in which increasing inputs of medical resources, at some point, produce decreasing inputs of acceptable longevity. However, there are enough prognosticators making their bubble reputation from some terrifying prediction about our prospects of survival. Macro-medical prognoses provide excellent copy for broadsheets and popular dailies, although much of it would be better placed alongside the Delphic utterances of their astrological correspondents.

I do not compete with these descendants of Nostradamus. In my professional life I have had quite a lot to do with the development of health economics, but only use this knowledge to suggest a framework for a series of tableaux representing the 'drama' of the dialogue between doctor and patient.

DEFYING DECREPITUDE: A PERSONAL MEMOIR

My wife Margaret and I considered how we wished to organise our affairs if we were to live longer than expected; our main conclusion was that, whatever effect longevity would have on our quality of life, we would want to remain together and, as far as possible, determine the pattern of our lifestyle. We realised that this was a counsel of perfection. We had seen for ourselves the particular difficulties that arise when one partner becomes less able to cope than the other, as for example if afflicted with blindness or some form of dementia. Our links to the social services would remain being tenants of a retirement flat. We would only too willingly continue as patients at the same NHS practice where we had been registered for over 30 years.

We would at some stage have to face the awkward fact that we would no longer have a car – that is, if we survived beyond the stage where we recognised that we might be a menace to other drivers as well as to ourselves. The list of obstacles to preserving our lifestyle could be extended much further but, being by now well past our golden wedding anniversary, we had learnt a certain amount about how to overcome or dodge them.

No advice is offered and no moral judgment made, although the reader may become more aware of some of the moral dilemmas that we all have to face in our relations with doctors and specialists.

Nevertheless, as I have already indicated, there is a bias in my narrative that is meant deliberately to offset tendencies in official policy formation not to take a more full account of the active part that elderly people could take in looking after themselves. Of course, older patients are encouraged to give voice to their reactions to the medical procedures that affect them directly, and regulatory bodies covering social services rely on recruitment among retired persons.

However, any realistic policy designed to improve the expectation of life and its quality must take account of the resource costs. This suggests an extended role for the patient as a 'co-operant factor of production' (to put it in the stark lingo of the economist). Innovations in medical practice are now putting considerable emphasis on generating information regarding the progress of an illness by using new technologies to keep track on changes in the patient's condition.

The presupposition that a patient wishes to remain independent requires consideration as to how far patients can act as monitors of their own health condition. 'Self-tracking' of the remedial effects of medicine on the individual patient is already a prominent feature on the research agenda. This fits well with an emphasis on retaining independence in old age, but this is in no way meant to cast any doubt on the immense welfare benefits of the communal activities that the old develop spontaneously to make life tolerable for themselves. I make no claim that this little book provides anything more than a starting point for the study of the organisation of medical services for the old, but it does take particular account of the wishes of those who in old age would like to continue to look after themselves for as long as possible.

I realise, of course, that having the chance to defy decrepitude is a privilege that many are denied by such foes as illness, injury or war. The fact that I illustrate the challenges of living into one's tenth decade does not mean that I am not grateful to have the opportunity to do so.

2. Living beyond one's allotted span

I was a patient of the head of the G Medical Practice, Dr A, on only one occasion. I must have been close on 80 years of age. After examining my record and going through that puzzling ritual entailing my attachment to his stethoscope, he remarked that I had had a 'good innings'. I was not sure whether this was meant as a compliment or as an indication that I had had more than my fair share of support from the NHS. My mother would have gone for the second interpretation. In her eighties, she announced periodically that she was living off 'borrowed time'. Asking her to whom she 'owed' this time and how she could repay her debt was not an advisable pursuit. It might have led to an argument about whether she still believed in the tenet of her Christian upbringing that one's entitlement to life was three score years and ten. Actually, she lived four years longer than my father and died at the age of 93.

However, it transpired that, whatever the scriptures may have laid down about the entitlement to living, Margaret and I were categorised by our doctors as among those whom they were determined to keep alive and in good spirits for as long as it took. At least, that was the inference that we derived from their treatment – even if no statement to that effect was promulgated. Let it be said here and now that we could not be anything other than deeply impressed by the results, given what GPs often have to endure from confrontations with patients who expect the Earth and from the meddling bureaucrats at their backs.

For most of us in the UK, the general medical practice (GMP) is the focal point of our personal contact with those who are qualified to ward off disease, cure us of ailments, and alleviate us from the pain of afflictions that will pursue us until we expire. The GMP is both a repair shop and a sorting office. As with relations with the local garage, the GMP can find out what problems bother us, decide whether it can cope with them in-house and know where to obtain specialist advice, and, if need be, transfer control over necessary action to the specialist's department. Of course, one can do without a car temporarily, by hiring, borrowing or owning another. In the case of medical action affecting our person, one has, as a client, to surrender oneself – albeit temporarily (hopefully).

A preliminary understanding of the process of seeking medical support for survival can be offered by accompanying me on a visit to the GMP. It is within reasonable walking distance and requires passage along a gentle sloping path. I know it well but the once-gentle slope now seems to me more like a steep mountain track, so I must allow double the amount of time than hitherto for its ascent. The path comes out in the very road where the GMP is situated. I can now see before me a church that is so trendy it has its website address painted in gold lettering above its porch.

The end of the path is alongside the entrance to a large cemetery; if I go in and follow its north wall I come out by a small gate opposite Y, passing the ornate memorials to Victorian worthies on the way.

Through the gate and crossing the road, I am at my destination. I am nodded into the waiting room by one of the invariably pleasant receptionists. They take one's mind off the reasons for one's visit, but only momentarily. The waiting room dispels any illusion about their greeting, for it seems designed to sanctify sobriety.

Two sides of the waiting room are taken up with notice boards that are festooned with flyleaves of varying size and importance. Today I count as many as 48. Collectively they offer warning of the hazards of remaining alive, and how to contact those who will rush to your assistance; these individuals are recognisable by some symbolic device but are covered by the familiar formula of 'if in doubt, consult your doctor'.

DEFYING DECREPITUDE: A PERSONAL MEMOIR

Conscientious study of each and every one of these warnings is enough to induce apoplexy – or whatever it is called today. Perhaps that is why I have seen only one person attempt to read all of them – patients seem all too aware of the dangers of doing so. The doctors and nurses probably know this, but pin the notices up nevertheless (because ... who knows? It may be a statutory requirement). Question: why not pick a 'priority notice of the week' and draw attention to it alone? I suppose that the choice could become the subject of fierce debate between members of the practice, already overburdened by paperwork and now asked to see if the paper can be made to work; a waste of valuable professional time better spent on seeing the oldies get their 'flu injections?

Over the years – as a patient of 28 years' standing – I recall various well-meaning attempts to provide the waiting room with some semblance of friendliness. I can vouch for its no longer resembling a down-at-heel Edwardian drawing room with an empty fireplace and sombre lighting. Instead of old chairs of various shapes and sizes and tattered upholstery, there are now cheerful cafe-type padded seats in pastel shades. Instead of the cast-off reading matter of the medical staff, recently at least one daily newspaper has been available alongside glossies in which our sexual problems are discussed with disarming (some might say alarming) frankness.

However, little seems to change the physiognomy of the patients displaying profound pessimism, although the scene can change quickly if babies chuckle and their older siblings play on the floor with trains extracted from a corner toy box. But anxious parents (frequently alone) seem to sense that sepulchral calm must reign and have recourse to unsuitable forms of bribery such as offering sweets to suck in order to induce their progeny to 'behave'. (I would love to talk to and make faces at these kids, but I have to remember that these days an old man with a runny nose can incur the suspicion of being a sinister paedophile.)

Surprisingly, the young adults, while often handsome or nubile, rarely display evidence of 'joie de vivre'. Their facial movements and body language suggest evidence to the contrary, until one realises that they are predominantly 'wired up' to mobiles churning out their favourite pop tunes. After a desultory look at the back issues of *SAGA* I retreat to my chair. The side door to the surgery opens and the young family are ushered through it, their chat recedes and we are once more enveloped in gloomy silence.

Now is the time for turning inwards. My reverie is far from reverential. I have difficulty controlling the agenda and I find today that I have caught myself trying to outdo my Fife friends in composing outrageous limericks about egregious citizens of their small towns.

Today I think I can score high marks:

> A young mathematician in Ceres
> Invented an infinite series
> When filled with elation
> At his own calculation
> His colleagues said 'you're ultra vires'

(Not bad – but oh so upmarket.)

I try to think of another way of torturing myself with a puzzle. Try reversing the meaning of hymns, constrained by the 'rule' that the metre must remain the same, as must the tune. I have never got further than the chorus of 'Onward, Christian Soldiers', and only then with a dodgy last line:

> Backward, pagan sailors
> Slouching, seeking peace
> Hoping the Jolly Roger
> Will signal our release
>
> Onward, Christian soldiers
> Marching as to war
> With the cross of Jesus
> Going on before

(Mm, last line a fudge, eh?)

I was never much good at reciting reams of poetry, only remembering about two or three lines at a time. I am now almost nodding off, conscious that an elderly couple have sat down opposite me fitting easily into the prevailing pattern of pessimism.

> I grow old ... I grow old ...
> I shall wear the bottoms of my trousers rolled

('The love song of J. Alfred Prufrock', T.S. Eliot)

No longer applies. Try again, Peacock.

> I have grown old ... I am growing cold
> The trousers round my bottom obscenely unfold.

Huh! A poor attempt at postmodern parody. Read your broadsheets and you will find that in the literary competitions, take-offs of Eliot abound – and most are much cleverer than that.

There is no defence for the enemies of decrepitude against the onset of sleepiness and, changing poetic gear, I nod off to Tennyson's 'Splendour Falls on Castle Walls', hearing 'the horns of Elfland faintly blowing'. Somehow their plangent tones are replaced by the voice of Dr C demanding my presence in the coven of consulting rooms behind the side door of the waiting room; 'are you ok?' he adds, understandably mistaking my somnolence for senility.

I manage to persuade Dr C that I do not require him to prepare a barrage of tests associated with such doziness, which might presage the onset of a heart attack. So, he asks, 'what seems to be the trouble?'. I am discomfited. I am not engaged in an act of imagination. I seek information that helps us in our mutual quest to keep me alive. Of course, I appreciate how much I owe him: getting me into the queue for the fitting of a pacemaker to reduce cardiac 'fibrillation', getting me to agree to stop smoking cheroots, and prescribing Warfarin (rat poison) pills for daily consumption. I know better than to waste his time (and mine) complaining about the odd whitlow or bruise.

I face him with my problem: having a life of itch as a result of Warfarin's side-effects. He agrees to allow me to continue to smear the affected parts with white paste, trade name Fucibet (no vulgar variations please!), only available on prescription and to be used sparingly. Dr C avers that Warfarin will soon be superseded by some potion or other removing the source of my irritation – *nous verrons*. Well, I suppose that elimination is eliminated and only the alleviation of itch apposite. It is being made clear that there is nothing much wrong with me, but no harm in allowing me to suffer from a mild dose of hypochondria. Or is he really letting me down as gently as possible by using a coded language that, when written *en clair*, emerges as 'good God man, can't you see that you have exhausted our repertoire of repairs; MOTs are a waste of money for old bangers'? No. I am rather ashamed at taking a conspiratorial view of his advice.

The sun has retreated as I leave the surgery and wish I had remembered to bring a scarf. The road home is downhill, if dusty. I return along the main bus route, but I shall walk: I have to, because I have left my free bus pass at home, never have the right money for the fare and the driver/conductor is not required to give change.

Still ruminating on my visit, I see the point of the psychological explanation of the desire to remain alive. So few of us are now certain that there is an afterlife or that we would like one and, recalling Oscar Hammerstein and Jerome Kern's song 'Ol' Man River' in *Showboat*, like its black singer, we may be 'tired of living but scared of dying'. So if modern medicine coupled with the Hippocratic Oath persuade medics to keep us alive, we have a mutual interest in remaining in their care for as long as possible. The head of G Medical Practice was wholly consistent in implying that I had had my innings. On the profound question of what happens after death I am uncertain but, unlike my intellectual hero, David Hume, I am unlikely to suffer persecution in this world from saying so. However, I would be dismayed if when I pop my clogs I were to be denied an explanation of the purpose of life. I have great sympathy with the taxi driver who, having recognised his passenger as the great philosopher, Bertrand Russell, asked him: 'well, sir, what's it all about? You should know'. Russell replied, we are told, 'I do not know any more than you do', leaving the taxi driver in a mood of surprised scepticism about the value of philosophy, garnished with deep distress.

Opting to defy decrepitude seems the only sensible course of action.

3. The perils of preservation uncovered

The scene changes. The quiet funereal atmosphere of the GMP's waiting room is exchanged for a large space redolent of humanity and recalling the lively atmosphere of a Hogarthian painting of cheerful metropolitan squalor. I am summoned to have a hearing test along with a host of others.

That is not my first reaction. That recalls actual experience of being a World Bank/UNESCO consultant attached to a 'mission' to Afghanistan to advise that country (in those days still a monarchy) how to formulate a request for an international loan.

Arriving for a formal meeting with the minister of education in Kabul, we found difficulty avoiding stepping on the bodies of countless Afghans lining the long corridors hoping to see him. (Apparently anyone had the right to an audience with him without appointment.) This was no ordinary queue. Every few yards would be a cross-legged group of be-turbaned gentlemen; some even sat round a primus stove boiling a kettle and sometimes produced a frying pan, remembering first of all to carefully return their stake money to the folds of their imposing gowns when breakfast took precedence over gaming.

It was explained to us that they were members of an isolated tribe for whom a visit to Kabul was regarded as an expedition and were not averse to staying a week in the well-heated ministry (it was December).

Some 'arrangement' could presumably be made with the porters to allow them to do so. The latter were also skilful negotiators of places in the queue, for which, no doubt, a scale of charges had been set. Our rapid passage to the minister's office was not obstructed, although at least one attempt was made to sell us a prayer mat.

A rather far-fetched comparison? Maybe. At least those of us who had received a long-awaited call from the outpatients department of the Edinburgh Royal Infirmary to attend for consultations were drawn up like three separate battalions labelled E (Ear), N (Nose) and T (Throat). There were narrow passages between each, sufficient to allow a wheelchair to pass without bashing the shins of their waiting members. However, there was a comparable element of bonhomie induced by propinquity and the sharing of a common purpose in view, namely how to obtain 'free at the point of sale' an apparatus to improve our hearing, we being 'E's. This might have induced me to pursue other parallels with Afghans seeking assurances about their children's education, but the hum of conversation, and the surprise and fun of the gripping tales of neighbours' accounts of their experiences at the hands of GPs and specialists alike, were sufficient to prevent the manufacturing of other ways to pass the time. I had prepared for this by bringing with me an article I had been asked to review for a professional journal, but now I had a good excuse for laying it aside as it was boring beyond belief.

In any case, a large notice on an adjacent wall assured us that we would be taken to see the specialist within 30 minutes of the time of the appointment. Dead on minute 29, I was called, gathered my belongings together and followed the 'herald' who had read out our names towards one of the entrances. I was expecting to be shown to a seat next to a specialist's desk, with a laptop on it clearly displaying my medical history dragged up from some vast mine of clinical data. No such luck. As soon as I was out of sight of the general gathering and through the entrance, I was assigned to a rickety chair on my right. Now I understood why half of the Ees had made no attempt to rush to the entrance when called – they had been fooled before. I thought of the notice as grounds for complaint; then I realised it had said one would be 'called', but said nothing about being 'seen'. A neat trick.

[Heard the one about the New Yorker who, on the recommendation of a friend, makes an appointment to see a psychiatrist noted for the efficiency of his practice? The front door of the practice is open and there is a notice above it saying 'come right in'. He easily finds a comfortable seat in the room before him and waits. Then he observes that he is faced with two doors, one labelled 'Gentlemen' and the other 'Ladies'. He goes through the first, finds it is not a toilet but another waiting room and by now he senses that he is undergoing a filing process. In this waiting room he sees one door labelled 'Age: over 40' and the other 'Under 40'. It soon must end, he thinks, looking round again when going through the first one. Sure enough, these are the labels: the first door is labelled 'Income over $250,000 p.a.' and the other 'Income under $250,000 p.a.'. He goes through the second one – and finds himself out in the street!]

I decide to try to doze off. A soft voice seems to whisper in my ear and it turns out to be an anxious enquiry from a worried old lady sitting next to me. She explains that where she lives is sufficiently isolated to regard a visit even to her nearest town, Kelso, as an expedition to the big city. She has only once before been in Edinburgh, and then as a very young girl. Two things threaten to overwhelm her. The first is what forms of manipulation or butchery of her person she might have to face. I reassure her that, if experience is any guide, the most she will face could be a specialist poking in her ear. That seems to help but then, after the ordeal of visiting, she would not be sure how to find the Kelso bus for her return.

Here I could not be certain but suggested that she should ask one of the reception staff, who were normally very helpful about this kind of difficulty. Did she have enough money for a taxi to take her to the bus stop? That at least did not seem to present any problem. This was the best I could do, recommending her to stay put in the queue rather than seeking to allay her fears of being left wandering the streets of Auld Reekie by going back to the reception desk to ask for guidance. She sank back in her chair in an attitude suggesting silent prayer. At last, an opportunity to seek quiet contemplation. I looked up at the wall opposite expecting to find a row of official notices similar to that in the waiting room at our doctors' surgery. Not so. A pleasant surprise. Framed coloured prints of famous impressionists? Not quite. They were all of one impressionist and gratifyingly similar ones. There before us were the Café at Arles, the fields of Provence, and the local worthies such as the postman and doctor. Surely these would appeal to a country girl, and drawing attention to them might cheer up the Kelso lass.

That was when I made my first mistake.

'Julie' – for that was her name – 'do look at those prints on the opposite wall.' She did and pronounced them to be 'bonny'.

'Glad you like them. They were painted by Vincent van Gogh. Strange choice for an ear clinic, *considering he cut one of his own ears off!*'

It was too late to stop myself. I could scarcely look in her direction now, expecting to find that she had faded away. However, the reason for her visit to Auld Reekie confirmed that she had hearing difficulties and some corridor noise did the rest. She had to ask me to repeat what I had said. Fortunately, at that very moment we were both called away to separate cells, where the consultants were waiting to examine us. A near thing.

This mistake was compounded by a second. It was early enough in the day, but already the consultant was hard put to offer a cordial greeting. My attempt to cheer him up was an abject failure. I remarked on the art exhibition in the corridor, pointing out the curious juxtaposition of a fine set of prints with the artist's self-administration of aural surgery. The consultant made it clear that he was not amused. Perhaps he had had his fill of heartiboots academics who made supercilious remarks and derived spurious medical knowledge from a quick shifty through Wikipedia before having privilege of access to his expert consultant services, which they clearly undervalue.

The consultant obtained his (unconscious?) revenge on me at the end of the tortuous process of assessment of my hearing deficiencies. I was presented by his audiologist with a surprisingly elegant small black box that contained a flesh-coloured appliance bearing a remarkable resemblance to a cut-off piece of human ear.

Of course, it would be stupid to generalise about the mood that overcomes specialists faced with patients attempting to be chummy and the presumption that the relief of the tension of the encounter should be pursued jointly. My long experience of specialists in 'lugs' – which, having a perforated eardrum from birth, goes back over 80 years – suggests that attempts to lighten their load through a bit of banter will fall on ... deaf ears.

Not so with ophthalmologists, it seems. Not long after the lug man saw me, I was obliged to return to the same Hogarthian scene on the recommendation of Dr C. (I had some sort of little growth just below my right eye.) I was called in almost immediately. Must behave *stumm*, but the specialist thought otherwise. I sensed that he was aware that I knew something about health economics, but I assured him that my views on performance indicators were ill-formed; we laughed at the thought that the NHS might now be employing economists to supply undercover agents with 'performance indicators'. He almost sought my agreement on the correctness of his prognosis and his course of treatment. Of course I confirmed his conclusions, particularly as it only involved another half an hour and no more than a local anaesthetic administered by his senior registrar. She turned out to be a gorgeous-looking creature with a beautiful husky voice who asked me a series of questions, noted down the answers, and laid me down on a surprisingly comfortable slab.

'Ah,' she exclaimed, 'I forgot to ask you if you are taking any drugs.' Then my mischievous nature took charge: 'Yes, one', I replied.

'Oh ... what might that one be?'

'Alcohol.'

'So ... I'm into that one too!', my prone position calling for her to whisper this in my ear – my good ear. Ah! It was hard to remember that I was only one item on an assembly line of clients. Friendly allurement, I suppose, was a technique for putting the patient at ease and a means for being able to stick to a punishing schedule. I saw no prospect of her accepting an invitation to lunch.

As one does, I waited anxiously for some weeks for the test results, finally going through the ritual of their retrieval from the pile of files awaiting the pronouncer of sentence on my fate, the big chief of the ophthalmology empire himself. His glance at my file seemed to have the effect of brightening his countenance, for it would only take a few seconds to assure me that all was well and maceration or myopia was not to be my lot. All that was required was some self-medication in the form of bathing my eye. Seemingly looking about carefully as if not wishing to be overheard, he lent forward and recommended that I use Johnsons' baby shampoo.

[Margaret didn't like to be reminded of this incident. At some later date, she had two minor operations for cataract under less favourable circumstances, culminating in her being almost locked in the Edinburgh Eye Pavilion overnight.]

These are only two examples amidst many others of the deployment of one's time on the specialist trail, which has covered clinics with similar rites of passage leading to consultations on the condition of one's heart, skin, urinary tract and bowels. As one's medical condition risks dominating one's list of conversational gambits, 'bomb' stories of World War II, numbers of holes in one on the golf course (important north of the border) and number of near air disasters avoided give way to claims to being top of the league in the number and variety of clinics visited.

DEFYING DECREPITUDE: A PERSONAL MEMOIR

[You will never fail to make a good impression with Italian friends if you begin a conversation, even with complete strangers, about your health. I am reliably informed that the same is true with the Chinese. I should warn you that the Italians will impress and maybe appal you with their depth of knowledge on what we would regard as unmentionable aspects of one's bodily functions.]

The obvious analogy in defying decrepitude dawns on one. You are likely an ageing car, a 'banger', that as it continues to keep you mobile, requires more and more maintenance. The MOT tests become more and more stringent. Not all the vicissitudes of vehicle preservation are reflected in the running repairs. What you may be repairing simply gives out. Hip replacement is analogous with detachment of the big end from engine and heart replacement. These are detectable and in a general sense predictable, as are such hazards of living as cancer and even epidemics. In short, it is difficult to avoid a long life unpunctuated by being an in- rather than an outpatient. Operations and convalescence represent further claims on precious time, the cost of which must rise perceptibly up to the point when the sentence of 'too risky to be operated on' finally has to be pronounced.

4. The questionnaire disease

'Cor! The parson's already on 'is rounds!' The char, frustrated in her successful attempt to entertain us with a mock belly dance brandishing her bucket and mop, ran off down the passage to the ward's rear door, deftly depositing her half-finished cigarette behind her ear, just as the parson came in the main door.

He stood for a moment at its entrance and counted us, glanced at his watch – it was 7.15 on a Sunday morning – and from long experience deduced that we were all feigning sleep. After all, we had been woken up at 6.00 am with a cup of tea and, whatever our condition, we should make some effort to be spiritually comforted. He bid us join him in prayer and we muttered our way through 'forgiving our trespassers' – I always stumble here because I was taught to forgive those who were our debtors – and asking to be delivered from evil. Our subsequent attempts to sing 'Fight the Good Fight with All Thy Might' hardly conveyed the spirit of its libretto, and would have made even the most cacophonous of dawn choruses sound like exercises in close harmony.

DEFYING DECREPITUDE: A PERSONAL MEMOIR

I then had time to recall that I had been rushed into Barnet General Hospital with my right index finger practically severed from my hand by an accident resulting from my failure to move quickly enough to remove it from the unplanned downward passage of a new stove pipe that my neighbour and I were placing in position in an attempt to improve the efficiency of our kitchen stove. I had been operated on immediately, and the combination of a general anaesthetic and sleeping pill made me unaware of my condition until the 6am cup of tea.

The record of my arrival and sojourn had not then been taken, but my kind neighbour agreed to provide all the details to the duty doctor early next day. It seemed to have been assumed that my neighbour had taken pity on some injured vagrant, unshaven, in clothes barely capable of achieving 'decency', and of no fixed abode. They were deeply suspicious of my claim to be a university lecturer, but when my neighbour expressed surprise and annoyance at their doubts, they rushed to my bedside and addressed me almost deferentially, anxious to know if I was comfortable and satisfied with my treatment. I assured them that I, too, was a recent arrival on the first rung of the ladder of professional advancement. When the specialist's rounds took place, reminiscent of a royal visit to the injured troops, he had already been apprised of my 'status' and asked me awkward, unanswerable questions about the condition of the British economy.

And the finger? Well, the specialist tried his best in three long postoperative sessions. True, my right index finger works but it does not bend – in short, it sticks out like a sore thumb.

I need hardly add that all this happened long ago when the NHS barely existed. In fact we have been talking about 1949. Some vestiges of professional privilege have and perhaps still remain in isolated pockets. A peculiar example comes from a decade or so after my Barnet Hospital visit. I was now a very young full professor of economics at Edinburgh University. Margaret had to have a minor operation and, being a professor's wife, was treated with illegitimate solicitude – or so it first appeared. The professorial specialist came in person to arrange with her when the operation might 'conveniently' take place. This was put in the form of a question: 'When, Mrs Peacock, would it be convenient for *your husband* to have the operation?' The context in which this 'joke' can be told has to be chosen carefully!

Readers may be glad to know that what follows is not a trail of reminiscences comparable with those in the previous chapter. Hospital stories are legion and the hospital sitcom rivals the police drama as the standard fare of television. You can play a nice 'intelligent' party game by taking my Barnet experience and listing the changes that have taken place in life in the postoperative ward since then.

As a social scientist – there are such creatures who are just as 'scientific' as natural scientists, sometimes even more so – one notes particularly the clear evidence of some success in treating all 'clients' as equally as possible; being an articulate person is almost a positive disadvantage nowadays, leading to the suspicion that one is 'too clever by half'. The NHS is, as it set out to be, the great 'leveller' of status when it comes to treatment that is claimed to be 'free at the point of service'. It is possible to argue, on the other hand, that what may strike 'oldies' are the similarities rather than the differences. The dedication of the nurses and medical staff remains, despite the pressures to maintain an ever-increasing 'throughput' of cases to fulfil some target reflecting 'value for money'. The professional cadres are still arranged in hierarchical form, justified by the view that skill develops with experience. As with many professions, scientific advance produces further division of labour so that the number of 'ologies' expands and demarcation becomes more difficult for non-medicals to understand. Alongside these developments has come an enormous growth of 'ancillary' or more 'complementary' services from physiotherapy to psychoanalysis and extending into specialised forms of nursing, adding further to the confusion of specialism.

The mere patient is not necessarily confused by the subtle ways in which fission of skills takes place. The simple problems arising at all stages of the daily cycle of events would be familiar to previous generations. When will breakfast be provided and what will it be, where is the loo, what are the visiting hours, what bedside medicines are to be taken and when, is their bed comfortable, when will they be allowed to go home and what postoperative instructions will be given to the general practice – and so on. In short, *plus ça change, plus c'est la meme chose.*

But not quite! One has to face up to the prospect of being afflicted by the dreaded questionnaire disease, which one is much more likely to encounter than some allegedly pandemic swine flu outbreak for which the hospital has been told to prepare.

You may feel lucky at having been picked up from home by some excellent ambulance crew who treat you like a piece of Dresden china, making you as comfortable as possible and then driving like the wind so expertly to one of those new wonderlands of modern medicine. You may not have noticed one ominous sign. One of the crew has a clipboard and carefully checks your identity and particularly your allergies. You are too busy thanking them when you arrive through some tunnel into the reception area to notice that these intimate details of your life have already been handed over to a receptionist and should be in the computer before you even see whoever is to assign you to a ward or operating room. And then you realise that all this recording will take place again, and again, and again. Naturally, you need to be physically examined on entry. Standing by the newly qualified young doctor assigned to this task will be a nurse with a clipboard, noting down your replies to a series of familiar questions. Pray God that you are compos enough to know that your knowledge of the English language may differ from that of the enumerator. He or she will assume that you are totally inarticulate, and you in turn believe that your inquisitor is illiterate. Let the system work smoothly, and do not try to enliven the proceedings with witticisms such as those offered by a Mexican student of my acquaintance who, when faced with the question 'Sex', wrote in the reply box 'Occasionally'.

And so it goes on from stage to stage. Next, the diagnostic unit – more questions – then the assignment to a ward, where the questions get more intimate and the clipboard seems to be getting larger. The realisation that you are not at your best in a postoperative state may prevent the onslaught of further inquisitorial sessions, at least until you are due for release. (By this time, your GP's pre-hospitalisation report may have been found, and you may be faced with assisting in the co-ordination of accumulated data so that answers are consistent. For some reason, one's age, of all things, seems to vary from clipboard to clipboard.)

You are not yet free for, as well as a statistical post mortem on discharge, you are warned that you may receive a follow-up questionnaire about your postoperative progress. Not now in control of their sample, the enthusiastic information-gatherers have to devise some means of inducing you to reply when you have escaped their clutches. Be on the lookout for two ploys. The first is that the questionnaire form is encrusted with official insignia that imply that any failure to reply will be to your disadvantage. The second is an appeal to your concern for your fellow sufferers, for your answers may be of particular importance for further research that will benefit your children and grandchildren.

Of course, I am a fine one to warn you not to succumb to statistical saturation. Medics and economists have this in common: they both appreciated at an early stage that conclusions about the human condition can only be drawn from careful collection and examination of data. The Royal Statistical Society was founded in 1834; its founders included Thomas Malthus, the best known economist of his day. The first woman was elected as a fellow in 1858: Florence Nightingale. Her famous contribution to statistical analysis demonstrated that the incidence of diseases in hospitals was influenced markedly by hygienic conditions, which was to have a major effect on the training of hospital staff and the organisation of hospital routine. She even invented a variation of the famous pie chart as a visual aid in statistical presentation, a technique employed to express statistics pictorially instead of blinding the reader with pages of figures. The history of medicine is punctuated with enthusiastic doctors engaged in community or military medicine adding a knowledge of empirical methods to support their diagnostic efforts. This called for some knowledge of entomology, given that insects were identified as carriers of disease.

[My own father, who began his service career in World War I as a corporal stretcher bearer and finished up as a captain in the Royal Army Medical Corps, conducted the first major investigation of the incidence of trench fever, a disease that had a major influence on the degree of incapacity of troops. His statistical data were body lice, and, not uncommonly in those days, he relied on self-infection to measure the progress of the disease.[1]]

Florence's proposals for the reorganisation of hospital services down to the design of hospital buildings, coupled with major revisions in the training of nurses, have a more immediate presence in what social history we remember. This knowledge extends to the vague feeling that she overdid it, which has provided grist to the mill of her biographers. First place as leading detractor of her effects is usually awarded to Lytton Strachey, whose main essay in his famous book *Eminent Victorians* (first published 90 years ago) is a literary tour de force. I re-read this when pursuing my father's World War I career, and was struck by two things. The first was that, in the last analysis, Strachey was bound to admit that Florence survived even his most critical observations to emerge as the outstanding Victorian of popular imagination. The second was that, even if he was not entirely unaware of her attempts to provide tangible results in reducing the mortality and morbidity rate of soldiers, Strachey made no mention of her statistical skills, including their employment as a device for improving public knowledge as well impressing professional medical authorities.

However, maybe a case can be made for the view that this aspect of her work has had the unfortunate result that diagnostic skills become subordinate to data manipulation.

Of course, Florence was able to use existing data collected for administrative purposes, which she then reclassified in ways that made them 'tell a story'. Statistical analysis has been extended with investigations based on samples rather than on complete 'populations', requiring a knowledge of sampling theory to check on whether some observed relationship denotes cause and effect. Thus, some recognisable disease may have several causes and treatment will depend on the relative importance of causation, as the statistician demonstrated by 'proving' that the decline in the birth rate in the UK was correlated almost perfectly with the rise in the number of issued dog licences. The devising of tests of significance to avoid errors of interpretation calls for great skill and commands great respect in the statistical profession. To have a disease that you have identified named after you may earn a medical specialist fame and fortune. To have a statistical test named after you can give you at least a place in the history of statistics.

What has all this got to do with us, you ask? You have to add another item to the list of tasks that are required of you in order to fulfil the conditions for being kept alive. You have faced the time costs of getting to specialist clinics, waiting there for the predominantly excellent concern shown for doing the best that medicine can offer, undergone treatment ranging from a simple jab to a full-scale operation for, say, a thyroid problem. Additionally, you are expected to be the unpaid research assistant to medical enquiries claimed to be of national importance – which might indeed be true. This is a further encroachment on the quantum of time left to you to enjoy the benefits of being kept alive that medicine is there to provide.

5. Journey's beginning

We come quite fresh to the different stages of life, and in each of them we are usually quite inexperienced, no matter how old we are.

Duc de La Rochefoucauld
Maxims, No. 405

Retirement is not death, although for my grandfather's generation one was fairly close to it if one chose (or was forced) to leave regular employment at 60. It has been common with professional people of my generation to assume that retirement is a stage in life when another (and hopefully better) life can begin; a springboard into a fresh pool of experiences and not a plank to be walked, consigning one to Davy Jones's locker.

Nor need retirement be regarded as living death, except by the few for whom working life was all that life offered or they expected. In any case, compulsory retirement from an occupation does not preclude some other form of employment beyond retirement age. The very fact that our health services are geared towards keeping us alive for as long as possible makes it almost a personal obligation to seek some form of daytime activity that helps others as well as ourselves. One can extend the argument to reach a high level of moral obligation (if not offering a clear path to reach it) simply by saying that to do nothing is bad for one's health and maybe that of others. *Basta*. There are enough oldies around anxious to offer you moral guidance. Stick to David Hume's precepts and let's start by asking what experience might tell us.

There is a small snag. Retirement is not something that is handed down off the shop shelf and sold over the counter with a guarantee of return of one's money if dissatisfied, with not much harm done and the possibility of trying something else. In making a mistake one cannot 'bid time return'; retirement is something not bought and taken but experienced. However changing tack is easier, perhaps, nowadays given the notable rise in life expectation; when the day of retirement comes, initial decisions are not irrevocable. We have medical advance to thank for that, and somewhere along the path to decrepitude we may still be able to change our mind. The loss of time may be a cause for regret – a 'disbenefit', to use a horrible economist's word – but is balanced by the expectation of making better use of it.

I am sure that several attempts will be found in learned journals to explain the logic of choice concerning retirement. 'Let alpha be the date of starting retirement and omega the date when you expect to surrender control over your time and effort to others.' God's truth, is that *really* what one might find in an economics text? The first time I came across it was in an essay by a clever, cultured graduate student who decided to write something on the economics of salvation. However, he had to extend the time period to 'judgement day' and meet the current conventions of using Greek symbols in suitably honed equations to arrive at a subjective decision rule. It was 30 years ago when he was theorising with tongue in cheek, but believe me today I am sure that there are journals where the satire of such an approach would be lost on the readers.

Yet most of us have to make some sort of calculation of the costs and benefits of alternative courses of action before the day of retirement arrives. Some will attach a high positive score to continuing to have some connection with a trade or profession where their skills can still be used, at least on a part-time basis. They acquire the advantage of a supplement to their retirement pay and remain in contact with a familiar social milieu. Latterly this maintenance of a connection with one's trade or profession has readily been formalised by its members, with provision for a whole range of benefits from free annual outings to discounts for everything from travel insurance to funerals. One can spend a fascinating weekend before retirement reading the now-extensive literature on a vista of privileges open to those who follow the advice of their pension providers, with the sheer fun of discovering what extraordinary opportunities are available swamping any consideration of the amount of valuable time wasted on this form of 'window shopping'.

The trouble is that once the news gets out that you are considering where to retire to and what to do, others suddenly discover a claim to be stakeholders in your time and energy. Children are anxious to know if you are within babysitting distance. If you do offer to retain a toehold in a teaching or research post, are you not the very person with the experience and patience necessary to supervise a few of the more recalcitrant or backward students? It is flattering to receive warm invitations to offer your services (unpaid) as, say, secretary to the local tennis club or literary society, or even as agent for your local government councillor. Universities may seek your services as invigilator of degree examinations or even as external examiner, a position noted for the paucity of its material rewards. Rates of pay and travel expenses are 'derisory', to borrow the language of the more publicly exposed union leaders. Even at home, your partner has already prepared a list of 'little jobs around the house' that have demanded attention for half a decade and now at last could be completed. As I write this, I realise that my *youngest* child has just become of pensionable age. So it would not be unusual if, on retirement, you have parents who would like to live in a 'granny flat' bolted onto wherever you decide to live. (The droll notice in the Italian *tabacchi* announcing that 'credit is only given to nonagenerians accompanied by their parents' might raise the expectations of future generations.)

It comes as no surprise that the mass of knowledge on which to base a rational decision about the dimensions of retirement is so overwhelming that it encourages eccentric behaviour. A shining light suddenly appears before the retiree, revealing the aspirations of one's youth such as the wish to be an airforce pilot (substitute engine driver in my case) or the crossroads where one took the wrong turning towards academic life instead of the road to some bucolic paradise where one could set up as a wine producer or even train as a bullfighter.

Perhaps longevity encourages the belief that one can 'bid time return' after all. I have known colleagues who took retirement as early as permissible and harboured the wish to turn their main hobby into a full-time occupation. One of them, already an expert on growing rhododendrons, even had the temerity to write about his experimental efforts, the results being printed in respectable horticultural journals in which articles must run the gauntlet of 'peer review'.

DEFYING DECREPITUDE: A PERSONAL MEMOIR

More adventurous perhaps was a professorial colleague who bade goodbye to economics in order to become an antique dealer. His professional training made him well aware of the risks, notably how to survive a trade where it would be advisable to become accepted as a member of the 'ring' (an exclusive cartel of bidders). He and I must have remembered the sad experience of the economics faculty members of a northern university who accumulated a mound of silver artefacts from a succession of sales of the contents of several country houses. They then organised a visit to Edinburgh to unload it, no doubt believing that they could have a splendid lunch and still leave a tidy profit to divide amongst their members. The offer by the first potential buyer was considered to be beneath contempt and was politely refused; a second buyer was approached, and then a third and fourth. They all offered the same price as the first! History does not relate how much was eventually raised. My adventurous colleague himself never found it possible to beat the ring or was able to ascertain the terms for joining it. This rebuff, together with a general fall in trading conditions, was sufficient for him to have to admit failure. He was bequeathed through this experience with a practised eye in looking for bargains and a fund of interesting stories, but it was all an almost unbearable disappointment.

But let me tell you about the most poignant example of risk-taking that has come my way. Professor X faced retirement at 70 and required little persuasion by his wife if not to bid time return, then at least to repeat some of its more pleasant features. As a zoologist, professional life was centred in the outdoors in the search for rare flora and fauna, but this seemed only to emphasise the loss of opportunity to enjoy the benefits of city life. Although he enjoyed teaching and had a sureness of touch in how to enhance interest in the life of the earthworm, the opportunity cost had been high in terms of the time that might otherwise have been spent on concentrated research on problems of parthenogenesis.

[Here I must interpolate the story of his one encounter with the popular press – this was before World War II – that resulted from their sudden discovery that parthenogenesis (or 'virgin birth') was 'rampant' in the animal kingdom. Arriving off the transatlantic liner at the Big Apple en route to deliver a paper at a British Association conference in Toronto, this very private man found himself surrounded by US journalists, who assumed that he was taking part in the ongoing debate on 'creationism'. They melted away when they found he was not going to talk on the veracity of Bible stories about virgin birth but about *sawflies*! One reporter remained behind and listened respectfully while the bespectacled professor explained how sawflies breed. The following headline graced the front page of some US daily the next day: 'Pity the poor sawfly: no father, no love life'.]

Professor X and his wife sold their freehold apartment, which provided just enough to buy a ten-year lease on a flat in Kensington that was within walking distance of the Natural History Museum, and also within easy reach of theatreland, parks and restaurants. It was at the museum in 1910 that the young, then unknown, impecunious zoologist so impressed some senior staff with his knowledge of entomology that they recommended him for the post of government entomologist in Nigeria – a wonderful opportunity to study the incidence of malaria (and to risk death from the disease). After surviving this experience, he risked his skin again when he was commissioned by the Royal Army Medical Corps to seek out the cause of the spread of trench fever in World War I. In 1917 an unexpected spell of leave was enlivened by the decision to get married; he and his bride married in south London and honeymooned in Folkestone before he had to return to the front. Time did not return to them, but memories could be relived.

They had a whale of a time for about 6 years. The emeritus professor was welcomed as an associate of the museum. His wife combined teaching Polish refugees English with learning Spanish. The metropolis was for a few moments at their feet, and they enjoyed rapid transit to short sojourns in Spain. (This was before the days when Benidorm was transformed from a fishing village into a mammoth Miami-like conurbation.) The Professor used to boast that he was responsible for introducing into Spain the innovation of having dinner served on a warm plate. His wife was an early pioneer of the discovery that the quickest and most comfortable way to negotiate transport from the ticket counter to an airport departure gate was by wheelchair.

It could not and did not last. They had miscalculated their lifespan and the cost of living. They learnt the hard lesson that to live equably in central London you must be rich or young but preferably both. It was hard for them to retreat north and to reconstruct what was left of life, but they did so quite cheerfully – not an easy thing to do when touching 80, even if skilled at forming new friendships. This was all the more admirable as the Professor lived until he was 89 and his wife to 93.

They were my parents.

Others spoke well of my father, even his students. Here is what one mature student remembered of him:

DEFYING DECREPITUDE: A PERSONAL MEMOIR

Professor A.D. Peacock: a word portrait

Zoologist: small,

  Animated,

    Bow-tie-tidy,

      A wiry bird of the old school;

        Straight,

          Neat of thought and act,

            Quick of foot,

              Eyes twinkling

                Generous,

                  Geordie-accented;

                    Perched

                      On a university Chair

                      He surveyed Earth's

                        Animals through

                          Round lenses of Oh

James Hall Thomson
(Artist, Dundee)

You may have noted a vivid contrast between the 'rational' approach to retirement suggested by a cost-benefit analysis and the examples given. A smooth trade-off of one objective against another, assigning, as it were, 'points to one approach as against another', assuming too narrow a content in which decisions have to be taken. Retirement can be the moment when 'opportunity knocks', for the fulfilment of long-cherished ambitions (completely changing the values of the objectives themselves). Equally, one may have reached a point where some long-standing obligation must be fulfilled.

In our case, our son David was the key factor. Severely autistic, he had been resident for most of his adult life in an Edinburgh mental hospital. In 1985, when I retired from academic life (but not from professional work as an economist), it was not certain that the hospital would continue to exist, and the form of accommodation suitable for his needs was still a matter of professional and political debate. It was only natural for us to wish to be more free to keep an eye on what was likely to happen. The location of our retirement was virtually decided for us, but one could hardly complain about being 'forced' to live in or near Edinburgh.

6. The dark shadow of decrepitude

The best-laid plans…

Given the hazards attached to making retirement plans, we thought the best course of action would be to take our time, buy somewhere to live in advance of moving back to Scotland, get our chattels calmly and casually collected and moved into our new *bield* (Ha! An odd Scots word already sneaks into our vocabulary) before Christmas 1984, and for me to quietly contemplate the various offers to have me suitably (but not fully) employed. Nobody other than close friends need know of our arrival. In any case the returning wanderer who nearly a quarter of a century earlier had given up a well-regarded professorship in Edinburgh for one in a new university, York, and later the only independent university institution, Buckingham, might justifiably be treated with circumspection.

The smooth transition to a quiet Christmas was soon disturbed. As we opened the front-garden gate of our new home for the first time, scrutinised by our neighbours' children, one of them pointed at our bare front window and piped up 'you don't have a Christmas tree!'. A bad omen; what else could one do but rush out, buy and install one? I pass over the litany of changes we were forced to make to our *bield* such as providing a short driveway to get our car off the street, getting the central heating to work and converting a store room into an extra bathroom. We were serviced by merry crews of lads who would, unannounced, disappear with their gaffer to other jobs, probably considered more lucrative than ours. As for the restrictive planning regulations, words fail me.

The hope of leading a life '*luxe, calme et volupté*' disappeared very quickly, or rather I succumbed all too readily to abandoning the prospect. As Margaret was only too well aware, the plan of inaction on retirement was a figment of my imagination. I had spent a fair chunk of my professional life as an activist, too interested in how economic analysis could be translated into policy, a sucker for starting new ventures in teaching, research and consulting – and quite successful with them – but manifestly too restive and impatient to be expected to see them operating in a steady state. She knew me better than I know myself or what I admit to knowing about it, and it came as no surprise to her when I reverted to type, the peacock remaining a leopard that did not change its spots.

A list of the items demonstrating betrayal of my very own intentions is sufficient to suggest how wrong I would be in neglecting to make any allowance for wear and tear on a human frame still in reasonable working order.

Item 1: 1985

Accept part-time professorship at Heriot-Watt University's Esmée Fairbairn Research Unit (EFRU) headed by Keith Lumsden, in former days one of my honours students at Edinburgh and now returned from teaching and researching at Stanford Business School complete with PhD supervised by Ken Arrow, who was later to become one of the first Nobel laureates in economics.

Keith's methods of working are best described as 'informal' but remarkably effective. He regarded me then, as now, as a kind of loose attachment willing to do or at least try anything he asked, and our relationship was sustained by occasionally vigorous but always friendly argument. In the first few years of appointment I found myself on a pedagogic rollercoaster that took me as far afield as Florida and Frankfurt, but I was unable to adopt that racy style of US business professors who impart the revealed truth about the state of the international economy with the confidence of the practised Presbyterian preacher. I was happier when I agreed to prepare a unit on government and industry together with Matthew Ricketts for a cleverly designed distance-learning

DEFYING DECREPITUDE: A PERSONAL MEMOIR

MBA that Keith carved out of his EFRU studies of programmed learning methods. While I am tempted to retell the history of this experience, all I need say is that Keith worked a miracle in overcoming administrative difficulties, including the cajoling of colleagues less adventurous than himself who were opposed to the whole idea, and understandably were worried about the need to monitor and supervise facilities for study in several parts of the globe. Now superannuated, retaining my professorial title – systematic demotion (i.e. unpaid) without loss of status – I bathe in the reflected glory of the pronounced academic and financial success of Edinburgh Business School, am still invited to (or allowed to) take my lunch in its excellent bistro and have access to those *Wunderkinden* who protect my laptop from my misuse of it and bear with my stupidity and ignorance of how to make it do my bidding.

Of course, some psychologists will tell you that (youngish) elderly couch potatoes risk the early onset of dementia and other inconvenient disabilities. Better to get off one's backside and play a regular weekly game of golf with your own kind than to seek to qualify and 'make the cut' in professional tournaments in which the prizes may glitter but are only within the reach of the young, strong and ambitious. I adopted a compromise of taking part only in the 'bespoke trade': I might be asked to write something for my peers, but I did not assume that I could keep pace with the young enthusiasts vying with one another to be head of the pecking order of professional reputation. It would not be long, I imagined, before I would be bamboozled by the *dernier cri* in economic theory. Like my charming senior colleague in my LSE days of the 1950s, Tom Marshall – famous in his time as a sociologist – I would be arriving one day at teatime announcing that I had just withdrawn my subscription to a premier academic journal not because I could no longer understand what was being written, but because my understanding did not even extend to the *titles* of its contributed articles! Even if that moment were to arrive sooner than expected, there would be in the meantime plenty of other worries, including the state of one's health and strength, to take its place.

So the seeds of decrepitude were already germinating in the worries attached to becoming aware of one's failing intellectual powers. Economists have followed natural scientists who have identified the onset of failure as cultivation of a growing interest in the history of their subject. I plead guilty to the sin of looking backwards, but have always found it intellectually stimulating rather than a consolatory sedative.

Item 2: a digression on activism

DEFYING DECREPITUDE: A PERSONAL MEMOIR

Before leaving my last full-time academic post, I must confess that I was really looking forward to a change of occupation more than the traditionally described well-earned rest, albeit one characterised by flexible hours and few responsibilities. I was chained to the idea of starting something new, and so it turned out. A good friend of mine in Edinburgh, Gerald Elliot, chairman of Salvesen's, agreed to throw in his lot with me to set up the David Hume Institute (DHI). I had asked why think tanks – there were very few called such in 1985 – were all located in London. Did Scotland not have the comparative advantage of a long tradition in political economy, perhaps best represented in activist thinking by the growing interest in the economics of law? (David Hume trained as a lawyer as well as becoming a notable philosopher who wrote some strikingly original work on economics.) We believed we could engender international encouragement and operate economically and efficiently. We would start with commissioning studies on the practical collaboration of economics and law, all directed towards improving the working of markets so as to fulfil the requirements of a liberalist economic and social policy. We would then hope to attract funding to provide in-house research but always with the desire to clarify issues of concern to those with an interest in public affairs. These were good times for me, with Gerald offering sage advice on the problems that would be of concern to the business world and contributing well-honed analysis both of general problems such as the role of takeovers in business practice and of issues that were some closely connected with his knowledge of shipping and fishing. Unusually, but equally effectively, he also advised on the economic problems of the arts. I acted as part-time director of the DHI for the first five years of its operation and was lucky enough to have Jock Snaith, former registrar of Birkbeck College, London, in charge of the office. The office was our link with public authorities, ranging from the Inland Revenue to the (then) Board of Trade, and with the various branches of business who expressed an interest in our activities and, in some instances, offered us welcome financial support.

I thought the right side of 70 was the time to hand over direction of the DHI to somebody else. Gerald, a great believer in not hanging on, wished to do the same and did so with a good deal better grace than I did.

Whatever I thought about giving up, like so many oldies I believed that DHI needed nurturing a bit longer – a foolish thought when I consider that my immediate successors were Hector Macqueen (professor of private law) and Brian Main (professor of economics), both of the University of Edinburgh. They had a much harder row to hoe. Devolution of government to Scotland offered more fertile soil in which to plant other think tanks, but left them more tied to the apron strings of politicians. Experience had taught us that reliance on local funding understandably entailed taking a particular interest in regional affairs, and it would be like squeezing blood out of a stone to raise local funding to consider wider questions of economic and social policies, even though many of these would impinge on Scotland. My departure removed any inhibitions that the DHI had about seeking public funding.

In my time the DHI did produce a number of reports on general issues, notably in examining the economic consequences of takeovers and the role of the public sector were Scotland to become an independent state. The takeover study was the forerunner of two studies, one on the loosening of regulation of the financial sectors in the 1980s and (more interestingly in this context) the other on methods of financing national health services. This was largely Gerald Elliot's doing. He persuaded the Royal College of Physicians of Edinburgh to join with us in organising a conference on the latter theme, an idea that appealed to its president, the well-known cardiologist, Michael Oliver. We obtained the services of that most versatile of writers, Allan Massie, to act as rapporteur, enabling the results of the conference to be speedily available. Allan's report (DHI 1989) is a model of clarity and was well received by both the medical profession and its more critical clients. My subsequent self-examination on how the NHS views the aspirations of its clients and how they react to it owes much to Allan's perception of what it is important for us all to know about the organisation of the NHS.

Conferences of this kind vary in the opportunity costs of the audience's attention. Medical specialists are busy people for whom time is at a premium. The anthropological observation by the speaker from Nuffield, then the major insurer of those who preferred private treatment, is engraved on my memory. He claimed that it is well established that 25 minutes into any lecture, half the audience's attention would have wandered towards thoughts of sex.

Politicians invited as principal guests at social occasions attached to prestigious conferences follow their own rules regarding obligations to the hosts. No post-dinner interlude to allow 'gentlemen' to smoke and ladies to withdraw could be expected at the dinner of a Royal College. The Lord Provost (a lady, actually) had been invited to our conference. Gasping for a fag, she surprised the top table by lighting up even before coffee was served. Not a word was said about it. Today, it is not entirely fantasy to assume that the police would be sent for.

Item 3: stop the world, I want to get off – but not yet

We had no sooner established the solid routine required of settling down to a quiet and anonymous existence when the temptation to partially destroy it was presented. I was called into the Home Office and asked if I would chair an *ad hoc* committee on financing the BBC; the committee's terms of reference were wide enough to embrace the wider question of the financing of broadcasting in general. Why me, I asked Leon Brittan, the then home secretary. I had an academic track record, three years' experience of government as chief economic adviser to the Department of Trade and Industry (1973–76), two calls to advise government on the financing of education and on the reform of pensions, and seven years helping set up an independent university, not to speak of previous encounters with the BBC on ticklish issues such as the performance rights of composers and the impact of their orchestras on the classical music scene. It looked as if I could survive the rough and tumble of controversy and, more particularly, refute the charge that I had been appointed as Margaret Thatcher's stool pigeon. (It was well known that she saw no reason why the BBC could not derive the major part of its finance from advertising revenue.) The economics of broadcasting is in any case a fascinating subject to a professional. I was hooked. I had no control over membership of the committee, but Leon put all his proposals to me for endorsement and I finished up, as it should be, with a remarkable team who would know how to keep me in order.

The relevant point here is how my generally good health would stand up to the shrill cries of the cognoscenti who believed that the BBC was the fourth estate of the realm. I was subject to surprisingly elaborate attempts to find out if I had anything in my career that would buttress a call for my removal, and the wear and tear of calling for written evidence and interviewing its providers, not to speak of organising a research team willing and able to make quick responses to the committee in the checking of evidence, would take its toll. I failed in my attempt to create the precedent of making our HQ Edinburgh and to appoint a secretary from the Scottish Office staff. This would have reduced the amount of wear and tear in travelling. The Home Office countered by recommending one of their own scientists for the post, and clearly he was a perfect fit. Even his name inspired confidence – Bob Eagle – and he was indeed a flyer who within days had persuaded the Home Office to supply us with a senior stenographer and typist and a computer operator. Mr Eagle did come to Edinburgh, but he hated flying and travelled by train.

We worked at breakneck speed and presented our report within the agreed time of a year from our first meeting. Broadly speaking, our conclusions were designed to improve the link between what licence holders (the main financiers of broadcasting) were offered and what they preferred. I still find it extraordinary that so much support remained among broadcasting pundits that the public should be the passive recipients of programmes supposedly devised for their own good. The debate continues even after 25 years.

The pressure may have eased off when I turned 65 (1987), but one thing leads to another. In the previous year, my involvement in national policies continued: I agreed to become a member of the Arts Council of Great Britain and chairman of the Scottish Arts Council. Thereby hangs another tale.

Enough said to show how easy it is to work on all cylinders for a stretch and then to find that if no allowance is made for the depreciation and maintenance of the human frame, one pays for it.

Item 4: intimations of mortality

There is no simple method for deciding on the moment when one is conscious of the possibility that, health-wise, it will now be downhill all the way. One can ignore altogether what the 'moving finger' writes and take life as it comes. This sets a trap for those who use this as an excuse for avoiding going to see the doctor at all costs. After all, the news may be bad and, worse still, you might find out that if you had gone to him or her sooner, the trouble that has finally driven you to the surgery could have been avoided. I suppose like many of my contemporaries, I am selective in my choice of ailments that call for a trek along the various roads that lead to the specialists.

If you have spent a fair part of your professional life interpreting statistical information for students, colleagues and clients, one tends to have followed a self-made rapid reading course in how to examine data, and this reduces the degree of puzzlement as to its significance that your companion at the breakfast table has to suffer. If you are compelled to give a quickfire reaction to her dramatic rendering of the worrying conclusions of some broadsheet article on the new hazards of day-to-day living discovered by some medical researcher, you are better placed to save time in its interpretation. (Or, as my wife would put it, measuring the plausibility of my quick response.)

Actually, the warning signs of the tangible evidence of decrepitude came from my dentist, a wonderful lady. Her waiting room was remarkable in eschewing copies of *Country Life* and *The London Illustrated News* alongside the daily 'rags', and offered instead *Radical Scotland* and occasionally sympathetic pamphleteering literature. (*Radical Scotland* actually had a new poetry section, and later I got into trouble when it was discovered that it received a small Arts Council grant.)

On her first examination of my fangs, my pride in how well I looked after them was badly shaken. 'You SMOKE,' she snorted. 'You must STOP'. My quick-response mechanism must have been in good nick. I replied: 'Let me put it this way, Mrs S: if I did not smoke, consider what other awful things I might otherwise be tempted to do'. She bit back any riposte and, as if nothing had happened, she demonstrated what a careful, skilful and sensitive dental surgeon she was. On the second encounter, she returned to the charge: 'I see you are still SMOKING! Have you considered being hypnotised?'. I expressed some doubts about this technique as a method of behavioural manipulation, but added 'if you are offering this service, please go ahead and let's see if it will cure me!'. Not unexpectedly, her reply was in a similar vein to her previous one. 'That's that' I thought, but I was wrong. Shortly afterwards, I was subjected to an in-depth interview on STV about my broadcasting assignment. Mrs S professed enjoyment of the programme but for one feature. She had not realised how unattractive was the array of my top teeth when I smiled and, not being able to quarrel with her aesthetic judgement, I agreed to have two of them crowned. (No further thoughts about close encounters with dentistry as practised by Mrs S and

Mr R, her worthy successor, occur to me: although the shape of my mouth and its contents have visibly changed, my admiration of their skills and sensitivity remain unbounded.)

The really significant incursion into one's life pattern begins when one has to both undergo surgical treatment and understand its consequences for postoperative care. One would be very incurious if one did not want to know what will happen to one under the surgeon's knife or when being internally wired up in some way.

Obviously, subjection to modern surgery methods has a profound effect on how one views the self-imposed task of defying decrepitude. Three experiences of my own offer demonstration. The first was the prostate operation only too familiar to males aged circa 65–70, which, fortunately, was successful. Allegedly it was carried out without general anaesthetic, although I am only vaguely aware of the manipulations that ended with my subjection to the humiliation of being attached to a tubular apparatus when I had to use the bathroom. This experience might undermine the courage one felt was necessary to face repeat performances by surgeons. Actually, it had no such effect. The unexpected result was that, having been a member of BUPA, I found myself in a private room, but I vowed I would never allow myself to be in isolation again.

DEFYING DECREPITUDE: A PERSONAL MEMOIR

The second experience began with my GP's insistence that I undergo a thyroid operation, although it did not seem to me to be a matter of urgency. However, the specialist who examined me and would perform the operation not only explained in detail what was involved but had that unique quality of commanding one's confidence that all would go well. I agreed to go ahead. He came to see me in the preoperative ward clutching a large textbook on surgery and, with a bright smile, remarked that he thought he would remember how to carry out the operation! It was a pronounced success. Only one thing gave me a jolt. I woke up from the operation in the intensive care ward and was shown how to give myself a whiff of quinine if I had a spasm of pain. I was relieved to hear afterwards that my sojourn in that ominously named location was purely a precaution applied in the case of 'oldies'. I was transferred to a ward with beds already occupied by a clutch of laddies of all ages who chaffed the nurses and persuaded one of the trainees to enquire from the charge sister the location of the acupuncture ward. An irate sister came back shortly afterwards, identified the ringleader and told him that if he did not watch out she would deliver a course of acupuncture by pricking the soft skin of his 'erse'!

It was some time later that I underwent a third experience that made it clear that I was moving out of the era when appointments at the medical practice were regular but infrequent, and now required constant communication, notably to add to the cornucopia of pills that are a legacy of the various attacks on one's body by the ravages of time. One is bound to notice, although not be given to admitting, that one begins to slow down. One probably doesn't mind if it is known that, after a prostate operation, one has ceased to go jogging before breakfast. (Actually, the moment of decision came when one found jogging to become obsessional, always leaving the house at exactly, say, 7.15am, following the same route every morning and arriving back home at exactly the same time.)

On holiday year by year in the central highlands of Scotland every late summer, the feasible hill climbs and walks diminish in number and length, until Schiehallion becomes too much of a challenge. The turning point comes when one finds that the rough path over the hills from Loch Rannoch to Glen Lyon calls for the availability of a car to return to the former because one has doubts about being able to make it back on one's feet. Our nineteenth-century forebears, dissatisfied with the type of Sunday worship in Rannoch, thought nothing of walking *en famille* over to the kirk at Innerwick in Glen Lyon each Sabbath and back again, a total distance of nearly 15 miles, all to hear a long sermon that was more to their preference. Their resolution, toughness and religious steadfastness makes us look a puny and wayward lot. By the age of 80, one reluctantly settles for the shortest carefully marked forest walk.

Then the day arrives when I fall down in the street – twice in one week – the only casualty being a pair of NHS spectacles. I am encouraged by the kind passers-by who help me to my feet to believe that our local pavements are badly in need of repair, the fault lying with the Edinburgh City Council. The cynical suggestion is made that our constituency does not have sufficient voters supporting the party in power, so we are far down in the queue for pavement repairs. I should sue the council for negligence. Another explanation seems more likely when shortly afterwards I have a dizzy turn getting off a number 41 bus and Margaret has to support me. Providentially, both of these incidents have taken place within 200 yards of the medical practice where we are registered. The practice calls an ambulance and I am whisked off to be examined by a specialist at the Western General Hospital. The stroke expert looks at me and decides I am wrongly categorised and, armed with his report on my condition, I am sent off to cardiology. The confidence of the specialist's judgement is confirmed by my having to walk through a long tortuous underground passage to reach this second port of call. At least this part of the 'treatment' is completed successfully.

Careful and sympathetic diagnosis calls for the immediate taking of an 'anticoagulant' tablet (Warfarin – familiarly known as rat poison), the fitting of a 'pulse generator' (a pacemaker) and a daily pill to counter 'atrial fibrillation' (irregular heartbeat). Wow! All turns out according to plan. The surgery in fitting a pacemaker is conducted using only a local anaesthetic, but I decline the offer of following the various stages of the operation that can be projected onto a large screen.

The reader can be spared further detail. Margaret, too, developed breathing problems that entailed a pilgrimage of visits to outpatient clinics that were even more extensive, exhausting and worrying than my own. Our medical history is of no importance by itself. We can claim it as not atypical, judging from the experiences of our friends and acquaintances. Even a cursory examination of the supplements of daily papers can reveal the obsessional interest of readers in their physical condition for which they seek the advice of a columnist with some claim to be a medical guru. No. It is the timing, the nature, the ordering and the seriousness of the illnesses that drive us to command the attention of our GP and his or her links with specialised aspects of medicine that offer the clue to the role we need to play to combat decrepitude.

DEFYING DECREPITUDE: A PERSONAL MEMOIR

For those like ourselves whose life expectation at birth seems to fit with our actual passage through life, there is some sort of pattern that determines the division of labour between our own role and that of the NHS in our attempts to maintain or maximise our enjoyment from it. This pattern changes as the more or less smoothly working machine reaches the 'old banger' stage when limitations – sometimes gradually, more often suddenly – affect the 'speed', 'distance' and 'routes' of travel. The analogy is useful but limited because one cannot swap the old banger for a new model, although modern medicine becomes more and more skilful at replacing worn-out parts through transplants. One must remember that even if we have some element of freedom in deciding how we spend our time as ageing begins, one discovers – sometimes to our surprise – that there are others claiming to be stakeholders in our future who do not agree with our choices of routes, speed and distance of travel. They may have a legitimate reason if they, say, are emotionally or financially dependent on us and we are liable to fall asleep at the wheel.

How one tries to untangle all these issues and tries to form a strategy of tolerable survival is the next step on the road. I have been given a 'leg up' to help face the journey – almost literally, in the form of a collapsible walking stick.

7. How was it in your day, Dad?

Age makes men both sillier and wiser.

Duc de La Rochefoucauld
Maxims, No. 230

Self-directed advice

The moment a walking stick becomes indispensable – a kind of third leg – rethinking is required on the relative roles of health services and one's own efforts to defy decrepitude. The golden rule is to hold fast to the principle of independence. You must specify the goals and identify the constraints on reaching them, and then 'bargain' with the health and welfare authorities on what is the best package of services that they can provide within their own rules of operation. You will never succeed completely in matching the means with the ends, but that is a characteristic of all forward-looking plans. The calls on the time you have allocated for rest, work and recreation may change radically, and your 'plan' must be flexible enough to allow for this. New discoveries or disclosures related to health expenditures may affect markedly the pattern of your prescribed medicines and attendance at clinics. In the course of a decade, say from 70 to 80, one moves from being merely 'ageing' to being 'old'. Consult a book of euphemisms and choose your own if you prefer to be, say, 'getting on a bit' to being 'of mature years', but the result is the same as far as the change in prescribed treatment is concerned.

Of course, you will become progressively limited by the normal wear and tear of the old 'banger' with which you identify yourself : your demand for changes in what it is expected to do cannot be matched to the reality of keeping it roadworthy, even in the hands of expert repair shops.

The extent to which you can 'bargain' with the health and care authorities so that they take account of *your* views on keeping you alive and contented is limited. Passive adjustment to what is prescribed as good for you does not necessarily ensure that the distribution of health resources is not biased in favour of the knowledgeable and intelligent simply because they can articulate their 'needs' in the lingo of healthspeak. Also, such people are more likely to be those who have the means to supplement NHS services with private consultation and treatment. Yet this may be the solution for those who wish to go on as long as possible using what brainpower they have left. The days, I hope, have long since past when one was obliged to take seriously the argument that NHS services were the main means to improve the distribution of human capital, and that the logical conclusion of this could only be that no one should be allowed to buy extra health services from the private sector.

Ha! Let's see this homily translated into action. One is bound to hit unexpected snags. (You can say that again, if my experience is any guide!) There is likely to be a gathering storm of circumstances that are largely independent of the essential help provided by health services and will call for a change in the direction of effort. Of course, ageing alone is an obvious barrier, brought home to me from my perpetual desire to have been a professional musician and composer. One need only think of the consequences for a woodwind player if he or she developed breathing difficulties, or for string players who have an arthritic condition. The position of the ageing composer is more complex, illustrated by the contrasting careers of Verdi – still at the peak of his powers in *Falstaff*, written when he was 70 (plus) – and Rossini, who claimed to have 'dried up' before he was 35.

What of the horny-handed sons of toil, the economists? Assume that you, like me, derive more satisfaction from continuing to write and argue in public than from retiring to some private fastness to contemplate nature. Your own training warns you of the price one must pay to continue to do so. If you are still asked to contribute to some ongoing debate

DEFYING DECREPITUDE: A PERSONAL MEMOIR

on economic policy, it is soon discovered that today one is expected to communicate by email. Incumbents of university professorships or heads of research institutes can pass this over to a fully trained assistant. Not so those with the prestigious title of emeritus professor who have finally been put out to pasture (although they are always welcome to visit their old academic haunts) and can no longer turn over their illegible script to a waiting secretary, who may even have regarded reading the proofs of the final product as a privilege.

There is only one answer: DIY. Fortunately for me, I had learnt to type (after a fashion) as a student and it was not difficult to transfer from an ancient Remington to a modern word processor. But more is required of one, for today's publisher is likely to demand print-ready copy and communicate with authors only through email. One takes a deep breath before setting out on the *via dolorosa* leading one to invest in a laptop and to learn 'pidgin computerish'. The nexus with the world of learning is not entirely severed. Lurking in the Adullamite caves of academic departments relying on numeracy are those who can be a very present help to those in trouble. They display a special brand of academic eccentricity: they are generally kind, helpful and generous with their time, and do not despise one for not being familiar with the latest jargon of their trade. They are even known to reveal some of its dark secrets, such as the remarkable effectiveness of 'switch off and then switch on quickly' when all else fails in bringing an obstinate laptop to heel. Such were and are those gracious colleagues without whom institutions such as Edinburgh Business School would cease to function.

Set on maintaining one's sanity, physical condition and companionship (now extending to over 60 years of marriage), it seems quixotic to continue to look for work if that is not necessary to maintain a modest lifestyle and enjoy a bottle or two of decent wine with family and friends. At a young age, it is a tragedy for an aspiring academic to clear all the hurdles of peer review of some prestigious journal in his specialism, only to have it turned down by a particularly influential and possibly prejudiced editor. Many years ago, I am told, two young economists wrote what they considered a breakthrough analysis in the theory of international trade, and to their astonishment had it turned down by some editorial 'guru' of what was then regarded as the top journal in their field. They drowned their sorrows and then consoled themselves by making a Plasticine effigy of the editor, in which they stuck pins. Some weeks later they heard that the very day they had tried their hand at black magic, the editor had gone down with mumps!

I puzzle over whether or not I have lost my self-respect in feeling more challenged by fulfilling a request to write about oneself instead of writing for a professional journal or a symposium. (Where one often finds that one can work to a fashionable, automatic formula: this is the problem I wish to investigate; here is a list of previous attempts to solve it contained in footnotes and 123 references; here is my alternative formulation of the problem and the appropriate mathematical solution: now observe how I test my results empirically; and conclude with a 'discussion' that defends, where it can, what one has 'discovered' but concedes that 'further research is needed' – and who better to undertake it than the author(s). Something of that kind.)

It is a great relief no longer to be chained to this mode of discourse, but that is not to say that some other mode will necessarily make it easier to improve communication between author and reader, once the author has acquired the rudiments of computer language. I did not imagine that I should have any difficulty in fulfilling requests to go down 'memory lane' (ugh). Alongside professional contributions of a conventional kind, somehow I had managed to write three shortish books using the 'bystander formula', trying to follow Margaret's insistence that one should minimise the use of the pronoun 'I', which would induce the readers to go off to sleep rather than stay on your wavelength. Still, it seemed to me plausible that having been, successively, a wartime sailor, the chair of an official arts council and a chief government economic adviser, perhaps I need not have to rely solely on imagination.

These musings fostered the illusion that I would find a ready market for further reminiscences; defying decrepitude, as it were, by self-indulgence.

Now watch a retired professor fall flat on his face.

Manifest failure

The deputy head signalled to the rector of the Grove Academy, Broughty Ferry, to join him at the window overlooking the playground. He drew his attention to a semi-bent figure skulking at the far end of the ground, nondescript but actually wearing a rather flash tie and twiddling his stick in a manner vaguely reminiscent of a drum majorette at an American football game. Who on earth was he – some sort of planning official or health inspector with a plastic identity card bouncing on his chest, authorising unannounced visits to educational properties? Or was he missing from an institution used by strange old men who take position in a playground and appear to be trying to emulate some football star by kicking an imaginary ball? Their curiosity was soon satisfied. Having spotted the onlooking rector and deputy head taking an intense interest in his ambulatory progress, the stranger made towards their offices and introduced himself as a former pupil at the primary school who remembered his days there, which were before either of the teachers had been born. He had never been back to the scene of his early triumphs and disasters.

The encounter ended in a promise by the 'intruder' to write a memoir of his time at the Grove. Just what was wanted for the brochure or whatever was being prepared to show the plans for the new school, which would be built alongside the gaunt purpose-built Victorian building familiar to my generation. What follows is the original text and an account of its 'fate'.

Immigration 1920s style: a memoir of the Grove Academy

The Grove Academy, Brought Ferry, where I received an excellent primary education, has been in the news recently. Their unfortunate pupils sitting their Highers encountered the unusual hazard in the examination hall of a plague of ants. I hope that this will result in some suitable form of restitution to the examinees. The school is now faced with a more welcome form of disruption – the provision of modern buildings to replace the rather forbidding Victorian edifice that has served its time. I was asked to offer a few thoughts for whatever requiem for their demolition is now in preparation.

ALAN PEACOCK

Our family arrived at Montague Street in Barnhill during the summer of 1926. My father, like my mother, was a Geordie. He had just been appointed Professor of Zoology at the University of St Andrews, a post held at the then University College Dundee. I was four years old and was sent to the Grove Academy when I was six – a year later than normal primary-school age – but was soon put up a class as I had learnt to read and write at home. My sister, Joan, was four years older and was enrolled at the Dundee High School.

In those days, although coming not far from the Border, we were like foreign immigrants. Academics were rare birds – especially Peacocks – and we encountered what seemed to be a foreign tongue, for then the Doric seemed to be something more than a dialect. Moreover, my sister and I had no religious upbringing and did not attend the Sunday school at the kirk like those who were to become our friends. (My father was to give some of the first adult education lectures in Dundee on evolution, which was regarded by religious bigots as a dangerous doctrine that questioned the biblical interpretation of the origin of man.) My parents' rejection of established religion did not prevent them from expressing (privately) their moral objections to my having to attend school on Good Friday, and I recall my mother writing to the headmaster, Mr Peterkin, simply informing him that I would remain absent on that day. But we were made very welcome – not least, I suppose, because my father, like so many youngish men in Barnhill, was a veteran of World War I. One of my earliest memories of Barnhill was meeting two one-armed fathers of boys who had befriended me. Sundays were a problem. My friends were marched by their parents to the kirk down the road, all in their Sunday best, and I remember skulking below a low hedge in our small front garden to avoid being seen in my old trousers, detailed to cut the front lawn.

To my surprise I have found some difficulty in remembering how I travelled to the school in Broughty Ferry. It was certainly not by bus, and it was only after I had been at the Grove for about three years that I walked home by Reres Hill and on the edge of the fields that still came down to its edge – a distance just short of two miles. But how did I get there? Then I remembered, and also recalled the reason why I had dismissed it from my mind.

In those days there was an early-morning train starting at Barnhill that stopped at Broughty Ferry on its way to the now-defunct Dundee East station. I have a permanent reminder of the journey in my left forefinger, where the tip of the bone was split as a result of it being caught in the hinge of the door of one of the carriages when it was slammed shut on departure one morning – a traumatic experience for a seven year old.

Once at the Grove I soon settled in. I have no tearful memories of serial bullying – although there were some roughs to be avoided – or of racial discrimination. Perhaps my musical ear helped: soon I learned to speak broad Scots, and my vocabulary was not so far developed that I needed to be bilingual. I soon became a Scot without realising it, and have remained so. My parents had a more difficult adjustment than I did, not least because soon I could no longer express myself in Geordie English.

I do not remember any semblance of class consciousness. Status in the playground rested on some category of prowess and not on which road we lived in. Being a good footballer or some such form of physical achievement, or being a comic turn – perhaps a raconteur of smutty schoolboy stories – were the factors that affected one's 'rank ordering'. My earliest memory of how to reach the top of the ranking would be something suppressed from talk outside the playground. One of our number, for a bet, obliged and astonished us all by being able to send a stream of urine cascading over the high wall that divided us from the girls' toilets. History does not relate how it was received on the other side. If differentiation of personalities made us interesting to one another, we were also bound together by two outside forces. The first was the school authorities. It was not that we hated our teachers, but that for a large part of the day we were in what appeared to be their absolute power. We could not be expected to understand how much we might later recognise to owe them when they were required to be strict and sometimes severe, if rarely unfair, in their judgment of our conduct. The second factor was the rival local school, the Eastern. To come through our rites of passage to early manhood required that we try to beat them at all inter-school activities and in occasional scuffles in the street, although I do not remember these reaching the pitch of the more dramatic activities of the Montagues and Capulets. (We then lived in Montague Street, Barnhill!)

Our teachers in primary school were exclusively female, all with very different personalities although uniform in their insistence on learning and discipline. Why, after 80 years, can I remember their names when I now sometimes cannot recall the name of someone I met yesterday? This is a common failing at my age but a constant surprise. At six my first encounter with pedagogical authorities was with Miss Hunter, who taught us to recite together simple poems, only one line of which I can remember: 'I like brown eggs far the best, picked from a nice warm haystack nest' (the words may not be quite right). She began the day by having us recite the Lord's Prayer on the assumption, no doubt, that we knew it already – not aware, I hoped, that I had never heard it before. She wore elastic-sided black boots. But, as explained, I was put up a class to be under Miss Mackenzie's charge, and she had the onerous task of teaching us our tables, which again were recited communally before we learnt how to write them down. Then to Miss Galloway, a nervous but attractive person, who expected us not only to learn how to write compositions but to do so in model copperplate writing, an art that I never mastered. She also taught us some history with a good nationalistic slant to it, which made me wary about betraying my Geordie origins.

Then in Miss Strachan's charge, by now we were turning into stroppy, outwardly confident youngsters, no longer the nervous tyros. But she knew how to interest us in our lessons, and actually entertained us occasionally with flashes of humour. However, another constraint entered our lives. A strap – the famous Lochgelly tawse – was draped across teacher's desk. Its occasional employment required the miscreant to come out in front of the class and receive whatever was the appropriate number of blows on the hand. This rather grim ceremony was no doubt designed *pour encourager les autres*. Boys (never girls) who were frequently on the receiving end of punishment claimed to have perfected a way of mitigating the blow by surreptitiously licking the palm of the hand before the blow fell, and then by cupping the hand itself. They would – extra-murally – proudly demonstrate these techniques to those of us who considered they might also be at risk of being identified as 'criminals'. In my experience, these techniques did not seem to work. I remember receiving two blows from a large-busted athletic trainee teacher whom I had irritated that were extremely painful. But the event I remember best was when, after a spelling lesson, nearly half the class of 25 or so ignored Miss Strachan's instruction as to how to spell 'woollen'. Those who left out one of the 'l's were lined up at the end of the lesson and she strapped every one of us. In later life I have been amazed to discover how often the second 'l' is missing in printed documents! But she was popular and we were all her favourites. And I shall always remember her dramatic versions of episodes in Scots history, from Bruce's stabbing of the Red Comyn within holy ground to her tearful account of the grim death of William Wallace.

I have tried to find a photograph of our mixed class at the age of about nine or ten, girls at the front and the boys behind. Having failed, I can merely list those I remember as good friends in and out of school with whom I swapped cigarettes cards, played conkers and football on rough patches of grass on the edge of the small golf course between Barnhill and Broughty Ferry, sneaked onto the Monifeith Medal Course without paying to try our hand at golf with discarded clubs, quarrelled about who should be centre-forward or bat first in team games and who would be detailed off as the Germans in our simulation of trench warfare. Disputes were generally patched up very quickly by some solution such as tossing a coin. 'Cogging' each other's homework came only towards the end of my time at the Grove.

Billy Cumming, Jackie Fisher, Ben Forbes, Ian Gunn, Peter Kinnear, Robert Leithead, Ian More, Bobby Ramage, Alfred Tragheim and Eddie Yuill ... where are you now? Yet I do know that Robert, a close friend, became a Merchant Navy cadet and died in the 1940s; Eddie Yuill, who like me became a professor (in his case in German at Aberdeen and later at London) died not very long ago. My departure to Dundee High School when I was 11 broke up the 'gang', and World War II led to further dispersal. I did meet Ian Gunn in Kenya as long ago as 1955, when he was a senior accountant in the then Government Overseas (formerly Colonial) Service; Peter Kinnear, my closest friend of these days, followed me to Dundee High and I saw him once or twice after World War II ended. I need that school photograph to identify the girls in our class, although I remember the Fleming twins, Betty Henderson (very bright!), Gwen McInroy and Betty Mitchell (another bright one, and industrious as well). But we were not yet of an age to be even mildly interested in their companionship or physical attractions.

But we did have our local heroes. These were the older boys already in the senior school. Those who arrived on bicycles were often plagued by younger ones gathering at the entrance of the Grove before school began and competing with one another for the privilege of taking their hero's machine to the bicycle shed for him. I seem to remember that there was fierce competition to take the bicycle of a boy called Royds, but I cannot recall why we thought so highly of him. I like to think that I must on some occasion have performed this service for George Thomson, later Lord Thomson of Monifieth, who became a prominent Labour statesman but was better known in Dundee as a former editor of *The Beano*. Many years later in 1985, when chairing the Home Office inquiry into the future financing of broadcasting, we had to meet as he was the chairman of ITV. His daughter Caroline, now a senior executive in the BBC, was one of my students who graduated in economics at the University of York when I was professor there. He and I talked on a number of occasions about the Grove, when we succumbed easily to nostalgia.

York jogs my memory about a last element in the fostering of whatever talents I may have had and that I owe to the Grove. York took its first students in 1963 and we made a particular pitch for mature students. Among our recruits was a recently retired pharmacist, Mr Crofts, who came to study economics and Economic history. He turned out to be the younger brother of Miss Crofts, who had taught music at the Grove so many years before. She was small and rather dumpy with a hairstyle that would not have looked out of place in a photograph of a Victorian lady. But she had a way of communicating her professional enthusiasm – and also I think a fiery temper – so as to make us work hard to please her by singing accurately and learning at a tender age not only tonic solfa but also musical notation. She had us singing two wonderful songs that, some years later, I came to realise opened the famous song cycle of Franz Schubert, *Die Schoene Muellerin*. As we got older she taught us part singing and entered us for a local musical festival at the Caird Hall, Dundee. Of course, we all thought that we were much better than the other contestants, and it is a tribute to the Grove that it mattered to us that we felt aggrieved at only being 'highly commended' in the judges' assessment. I nearly lost my place in the choir by singing too loudly but pleaded to be allowed to remain in it, learning the important lesson that the effectiveness of communal activity depends on trust and compromise.

I cannot recall why my parents decided to send me to Dundee High School, which was known disparagingly at the Grove as 'the Dundee Hot Scones' and other probably unrepeatable epithets. It may have been something to do with the curriculum available at the time. I was then just 11, and certainly

DEFYING DECREPITUDE: A PERSONAL MEMOIR

had no choice in the matter. Published memoirs of childhood are frequently replete with accounts of the sufferings of the young undergoing the pains of adolescence, usually endowed with unfeeling parents who have left them to the mercies of cruel, cynical and equally unfeeling teachers whose only weapon against the horrors of instilling knowledge into their seemingly brainless charges being cynical mental torture coupled with sadistic punishment.

That was certainly not my experience, and I settled happily enough at Dundee High. I am sure that I owe this in large part to my mentors at the Grove and having the opportunity to learn there how friendships are formed – and how they are to be kept.

© Alan Peacock 2007

I had taken some trouble over the text, but I made it clear when I submitted it that I would be glad to make any changes to shorten or amend the article. I did not think for one moment that it would be rejected out of hand. I waited and nothing happened, and supposed that the text had gone missing. I rang the school, was told that they had received the script and would be getting in touch with me about it. Over four years later, I am still waiting for a reply! I tried it out as a possible contribution to one of the several Scots periodicals that offer their authors the chance to lament the death of our glorious past. I received a curt letter of rejection implying that I had written a piece of pornography. I sent the manuscript to friends who would not be averse to pulling it apart, not one of whom believed that my account of my first impressions of the Grove could give offence. There was a suggestion in one verbal comment that writing in a style in consonance with that of contributors to *The Oldie* would not necessarily appeal to the burghers of Broughty. My grandson could find nothing unusual or objectionable in my story of the urinary competition, but was outraged by the use of the tawse. It was not clear to me why he thought that this was an argument for toning down the passage about punishment. Reading through what I said and comparing it with a personal perception of the expectations of those who would encounter it in a school magazine or separate appeal for cash, I suppose I have to admit that it is hardly 'fit for purpose'.

This experience was a warning that maintaining one's competitive position as something of a scholar with activist pretensions when one has reached 80 plus required much closer attention to the nature of the 'market'. I had been writing for dailies and periodicals and undertaking consulting work by invitation for over half a century, but found it hard to accept that I now worked at a slower pace and against declining expectation that I had anything to say. Of course, the simple solution was for me to retire altogether so that

DEFYING DECREPITUDE: A PERSONAL MEMOIR

Margaret and I need not tie our leisure hours to some invitation received to give economic advice in some distant land. I was not made that way, and some further practice in writing about 'how it was' still commanded some attention, and there were actually some younger colleagues who continued to persuade me to contribute to their research. So I had not quite reached the stage where I would only be useful as an obituarist because there were so few of my generation who were still alive. As it was, I retained a vivid memory of that remarkable scientist, Sir D'Arcy Thompson (renowned author of the pathbreaking *Growth and Form*), my father's senior colleague, who waved me to a chair beside his desk where he was tapping out on an aged 'sit up and beg' typewriter what turned out to be the obituary of a departed colleague. D'Arcy was almost rejoicing in the fact that he was the only one left who knew enough about him to perform this necessary task. And here was I almost exactly the same age as D'Arcy was then.

First encounters with medical education

Inevitably, then, the process of ageing means a change in working practices, notably in trying to prevent the balance of activity moving too quickly in one direction of time spent on one's physical preservation (and therefore visiting the surgery or hospital clinic, or at least finding oneself being taught about self-medication symbolised in the need to read more carefully the instructions on the medicine bottle!). While this has meant a diversion explaining how continuing to write what is meant to be read might require quite a change in style, a suitable place to end the chapter is to recall an early encounter with medical education that actually took place when I was in my last year at the Grove.

Eddie Yuill and I had been, like the rest of the class, confronted by a small, earnest young man who was invited to replace Ms Strachan for one period because of the importance of his message to us. He was some sort of itinerant lecturer supplied by an organisation known as the Band of Hope (BoH) whose purpose was to convince young and old of the dangers of drink, although not insisting that salvation required total abstinence. (I suppose my ignorance of the existence and purpose of the BoH was the result of the non-attendance of my family at church.) The lecturer spoke well, produced coloured anatomical charts to describe the corroding effects of alcohol on the human frame, and obtained permission for us all to have an afternoon off in order to view the physical manifestation of these effects as pickled in several glass jars on display in an exhibition at the BoH Dundee premises. It was most enjoyable, rather like seeing a horror film – and free, too. (Not quite: only a day or two later we had to spend our next essay period writing on 'The Dangers of Drink', hardly regarding the award of prizes by the BoH for the best two essays as adequate compensation.)

Of course, Eddie got the first prize alongside his normal quantum of books for being top of the class for his year. I received my usual 'good progress' volume of piano pieces but that did not count, music being an extramural pursuit. However, to my surprise, I received the second prize awarded by the BoH. My reward was a puzzle: a copy of a now-unknown novel by Arthur Conan Doyle called *Uncle Bernac*, which began with an account of the techniques used to smuggle French brandy into England at the time of the Napoleonic Wars. Even more puzzling was Eddie's reward: a nice edition of Dickens' *Tale of Two Cities* in which, as we all know, the hero Sidney Carton is an alcoholic. The subtlety of these choices as a way of furthering the aims of the Band of Hope eluded me and my parents, who were vastly entertained by the award.

8. 'The strife is o'er … the battle lost'

So decrepitude cannot be staved off, at least for long, and its onset can take various forms that are all too familiar. Positive action to defy it becomes more and more problematic because that means estimating the pace of wear and tear, over which we have little control. I find my contemporaries who speculate on their own life expectation more interested in each other's pattern of medical history than in age differences. So X looks in worse condition than Y because of some, say, genetic difference. Or A 'popped his clogs' well before his twin B, the result of self-induced lung cancer, one being a smoker and the other a non-smoker. In any case whatever control can be exercised over our physical decay, tied to a wish to live longer in reasonable comfort, we find ourselves in more frequent contact with medical practice. The price of comfort rises as we make allowance for the extra time now to be taken up by visits to the GMP, clinics and hospitals. Medical attention is no longer to be regarded as some form of regular oiling of the remaining moving parts of the human machine. Its form, availability and effectiveness change completely, and often very suddenly, the general pattern of our daily lives. The 'bystander' attitude that has allowed me to present contact with health services as a series of more or less *conversazione* must be laid aside. The future will not be a replication of the past. Having reached octogenarian status, one finds that the ditty 'old soldiers never die, never die, never die ... they simply fade away' is a treacherous guide to our fate.

It may be difficult to formulate a satisfactory principle of independence, but one can still identify what it entails for the practical business of living. Margaret and I may have had daily disagreements about everything from the choice of meals to which TV news channel would close off the day for us, but we discovered early in married life that, to our constant surprise, we had much in common when it came to crucial decisions. The first of these concerned living quarters. We were anchored in Edinburgh and would remain so, and live together, come what may. In practical terms that meant a minimum of two bedrooms (to allow for inconvenient illnesses), sitting room, bathroom and kitchen. Margaret much preferred a narrow kitchen that had lots of inlaid cupboards and room only for the chef (known vulgarly as an OBG (one-bum galley)).

In fact, I have described a fairly typical retirement apartment of the kind that are occupied by approved tenants of some form of private or local-government housing scheme, but we soon discovered that there are many variants. If you feel inclined to look for similar accommodation, read the contract between owner and tenant carefully! I have seen examples where the duties of tenants are set out in detail and read like army orders of the day, whereas there is little mention of tenants' rights. Fortunately, the networking of academic retirees was well developed, and we found an apartment in a retirement 'complex' (as they are labelled) that was compatible with our prognosis of means, environmental preferences and growing decrepitude.

Advanced thinking about the 'needs' of the old emanating from professional bodies (ranging from doctors to dieticians) seemed to favour domiciliary location, though not necessarily regular home visits from members of a medical practice. However, assigning as we did a high value to our independence, our approach pointed towards a different direction, and one that is counter to the rapid technological changes affecting domestic life. For example, it is all too easy to locate the website of a well-known supermarket offering a myriad of prepared foods, draw up a list of those that you would like to sample and submit your order. Your choices can be delivered to your door and paid for electronically. And so domestic shopping now extends to such a wide range of consumer goods and even personal investment items – anything from pianos to patios – with the only physical activity required of the purchaser being to answer the doorbell. Such convenience is the enemy of independence and reduces the resistance to passive adjustment to one's personal environment. Of course, one's degree of mobility is itself dependent on one's physical condition, but before that becomes a limiting factor, it is all too easy to succumb to the temptations of obtaining service without direct personal communication.

One obvious way to keep sufficiently au fait with the routine of ordinary life was to hold on as long as possible to a car. This certainly reduced the time costs of keeping in touch with those whose company one wished to continue to enjoy, allowing one close inspection of goods and products at the point of sale, and the necessary propinquity to those with whom one wanted to discuss and debate local and national policy matters and to join in helping others.

The organisation of retreat

But like so many ways open to maintain direct human contact, one by one obstacles obtrude to reduce such opportunities. It is all too easy to overestimate one's prowess as the family chauffeur. The day comes when the car must be sold or given away. I remember that day all too well. My cautious son, Richard, expressed willingness to take over our almost-new Agila, but not before conducting a minute inspection of its roadworthiness. If we had not known him better, we might have discerned a note of condescension in his acceptance. After all, your old dad might have forgotten to fill the tank and would not know how to read the oil gauge. A trial run brought a nice smile to his face and warm approval.

The signs are clear. At some point one discovers that one is looking at the signal for retreat. From now on the pattern of life can no longer be shaped by those remaining intellectual, psychological and physical capacities that have enabled one to satisfy one's desire for keeping in touch with the outside world. Of course, this comes as no surprise to anyone who already suffers from some chronic illness and is already warned of its influence on one's remaining length of life. The concern here is more with the general organisation of retreat that all of us have to face as the 'old banger' grows in vulnerability and rusts away.

I have learnt to be impressed by the stern resistance displayed by ageing ladies of the middle class, so often the butt of jokes about their haughty manner, narrow perspective on cultural matters and bland assumption that nothing of any consequence happens beyond the confines of Edinburgh. Gingerly open the door leading into a church hall of an afternoon, and you may believe that your prejudices are confirmed by the rituals of the bridge table that dominate the scene. You tiptoe backwards and hope the door does not creak as you sneak away, convinced that you had just avoided being snarled at by the occupants of this lioness's den.

How wrong you may be. You might have had time to notice that the age range could be as much as 30 years (from 65 to 95), that at every second table there is a wheelchair, and that walking sticks are much in evidence. (Margaret was only able to remain a member of one of these gatherings because a helpful neighbour gave her a lift by car.) Several bridge companions, as well as coping with their own growing infirmities, had ailing husbands or relatives to care for. If a member of the club was clear of such responsibilities, likely as not they would assume others – such as being a voluntary helper in a hospice, charity shop or church. In short, the defiance of decrepitude becomes a communal activity and offers a pointer to what is likely to emerge as the pattern for the future when the 'burden' of an already ageing population cannot be sustained by the working population alone. *The ageing assume a growing responsibility for the welfare of the aged.*

By now well into our 80s, Margaret and I did not wish to wait around until policymakers devised ways of 'building' on this disposition of the aged to combine self-help with mutual aid. There were plenty of signs already that politicians with an urge to do good (as well as doing well for themselves) could favour some regimentation of the aged into 'complexes' that would 'rid' them of the 'worry' of making their own plans. Thus we were glad to have the companionship of other tenants in our retirement complex but also to have the freedom of choice that goes with a wish to be independent. We formed a close tie with an independent care agency that left us to decide what kind of help would supplement our own efforts and provided a reliable service of experienced helpers.

How long have I got?

Our plan seemed to work well. Like all plans with any claim to provide action to be taken, they had to be revised almost weekly. For instance, a more or less monthly check-up on my intake of Warfarin might lead to changes in the dose and possible adjustment in other medicines among what appeared to be a growing cornucopia of pills. Patients were well advised to know the relationship of one form of medicine to another; that is, would read, understand and apply the instructions on the pill container, with the added problem that 'oldies' might not be sure whether or not they had adhered to the correct dosage. That presented us with few worries, but applied generally to medical practice, it assumes that specialists and doctors are correct in both diagnosis and prognosis. No guarantee or infallibility was expected but, with those of advanced age, fighting for the time to enjoy a postulated increase in one's life expectation required some indication of how long we had to live. This might come down in practical terms to knowing whether any course of treatment was designed to cure or to simply alleviate some condition affecting our welfare.

An answer to this last question can present a poignant difficulty in communication between medicals and aged clients. First, the question in the mind of the client is always 'how long have I got, doctor?' but, even if one is endowed with self-awareness and courage, the client's fear of the answer is sufficient to prevent the question from even being put. Second, there can be a corresponding inhibition on the part of the GP or specialist to provide an answer. Normally, he or she has to know the client/patient well before deciding whether to answer the question as put or whether to avoid answering it at all, even assuming that they are confident that their prognosis can be sufficiently precise. One can understand any hesitation on behalf of highly experienced heads of specialist clinics at even sketching out the future progress of some terminal medical condition and how best to face it, given the miniscule amount of clinical time that can be allocated to studying the medical history of any individual patient.

As I have mentioned, Margaret suffered from emphysema and knew that it was incurable. She considered herself lucky to be able to refer her worries about the progress of the disease to one particular doctor in the practice we attended. As occasion demanded, I took her to the specialist clinic in the Royal Infirmary of Edinburgh and there, I believe after the third such visit, the head of the clinic asked us both to be present at his consultation and, without hesitation, simply told us that his team and our doctor had done all that was possible to prevent further deterioration in Margaret's condition. Cure was impossible but methods of alleviation were available and improving. It was hard to take. Our reactions took time but were identical. We were immensely impressed with the sensitive way in which the news was broken and the clear indication that while they could do no more, in other respects they would do what was possible. We recalled together another occasion when we had to face a medical judgement. We appeared before a panel of psychiatrists at the Maudesley Hospital no less than 60 years earlier to be informed that our son, David, was an incurable 'imbecile'. The news was delivered as if it was a 'guilty' verdict. A psychiatric social worker was at hand to 'advise' the shattered parents. (Actually, David has proved to be severely autistic, but the word had hardly entered the ornate vocabulary of psychiatry in 1950. His abstract paintings have been much admired.)

DEFYING DECREPITUDE: A PERSONAL MEMOIR

The visible manifestations of 'defeat' are clear to any reasonably observant person. In a retirement complex, a little world on its own, everyone can know what is happening but that need not undermine discretion. Thus, a domiciliary visit by a doctor will be something of an event given that the usual patient contact is at the surgery, which is not far away ('that'll be Margaret...'). Margaret did appear, maybe to sit on a chair by our front porch, and armed with one of those improved three-wheeled Zimmer frames had been known to make it to the local store by herself. In time, at the behest of the doctor, other curiosities of equipment were delivered by yet another branch of the NHS, usually at unusual times such as the weekend. Every week a sprightly youth arrived from the chemist with prescribed medicines in a packet that seemed to grow in size week by week. The telltale item was an article that looked like a prop from *The Illness of George III*. I was so appalled that I arranged to buy something more comfortable. I spent as much time as possible with Margaret and we managed to get out a bit. We were driven by Jim Marriott, who runs a one-man taxi firm, is a good friend and knows precisely where we can obtain any domestic article. The ironic twist to this account of defying decrepitude is to be found in the last time Margaret and I shopped together – to buy a de luxe commode.

The doctor advised us to have a short period of respite care whereby Margaret would be transferred to the nearby care home, where everything is done for the resident; the inference was drawn by our fellow tenants that she would remain there. For those who have become severely physically disabled or have dementia this may be the answer, but our separation, even for a week, was an ordeal rather than a relief, somewhat to our surprise. But our splendid doctor saw a way out. Advantage could be taken of a new development in domiciliary treatment in which someone like Margaret, after a few days' training, could look after her own medication, including the administering of morphine. It entailed a short stay in the Marie Curie Hospital, Edinburgh, and as luck would have it a bed was available immediately. There was no need for Margaret to begin packing; she was packed already. Like an experienced refugee, all too ready to move on at a given signal, she extracted a grip from a bedroom cupboard. We rang, as instructed, for an ambulance. The demand for ambulances stretched far into the distance of time with no prospect of supply meeting demand, so our niece Caroline, that very moment arriving for a short visit, immediately offered to take us. There was just enough room for us and the grip, Caroline insisting on leaving her 'unpacking' until later. There can be nothing strange about a puppeteer like Caroline forgetting to warn you not to sit on two of her creations, in need of repair and occupying the back seat. The presence of a small blind dog snoring away under a blanket is another matter. That made our arrival at the Marie Curie somewhat unusual, if unforgettable.

Margaret arrived on a Monday. The combination of what was clearly expert medical attention and the sympathetic understanding of the staff was overwhelming. Relatives were not shooed away with visits only made during prescribed hours, strictly kept, but were treated as a member of the 'team' responsible for Margaret's care. She quickly and visibly relaxed and the true extent of the exhausting and prolonged struggle that her condition had demanded was thereby revealed. She was brilliantly looked after; she fully appreciated this and indicated her gratitude, but I think we had all overestimated her strength. Early on Friday 4 November, she died in her sleep.

A volunteer helper of the night staff made herself known to me as one of those who had nursed Margaret, giving me the opportunity to offer profuse thanks and to ask her what I could do in return. She replied 'my reward is having had the opportunity to have nursed that splendid lady, Margaret'. Coming from a stiff-upper-lip family, I was hard put to it not to weep.

9. Defiance gives way to resignation

When you cannot find your peace in yourself it is useless to look for it elsewhere.

Duc de La Rochefoucauld
Maxims, No. 571

Once having faced up to and undergone the uncontrollable influences on one's life inevitably associated with the death of a very dear person, one was tempted to abandon the principle of independence. NO. That would be cowardly, tough though one finds being without a partner of nearly 68 years and with defying decrepitude bound to get more and more difficult.

In fact, thinking what to do next is a necessary element in trying to put bereavement behind one. One begins, like Sir Bedevere in Tennyson's *Morte d'Arthur*, and thinks 'whither shall I go? For where shall I hide my forehead and my eyes? For now I see that the true old times are dead'. Such sentiments may evoke sympathetic responses from neighbours, most of whom are widows or widowers, but they are understandably cautious about offering specific suggestions.

DEFYING DECREPITUDE: A PERSONAL MEMOIR

Sprach Peacock to himself but fortunately, so far, silently. Why this sudden breakout into quotes and dubious literary flourishes, already displayed in this slim volume? A relic of trying to pass school examinations by memorising a few nice phrases in the hope it would lead the examiners to believe that I had actually read the literature that supplied them, I suppose. As already demonstrated, I find the recall and personal variation of quotations a way of passing the time while waiting my turn at the doctors' surgery. But I would be doing myself less than justice by making this habit the first port of call to get advice on how long and in what manner I could continue to defy decrepitude. That's not what the principle of independence stood for.

The reactions of those who suffer bereavement or comparable after-shock are often way out of line with the expectations of even their close friends, far less their neighbours. In the past, it was reflected in my own family in an uncontrollable desire to make radical and rapid changes in their domestic furniture – not by any means an uncommon reaction. Margaret and I, it so happens, had been making plans for getting rid of three large items, particularly the three-cushion sofa in our tiny living room that already contained an upright piano. Of course, the piano could not go so the sofa was to be replaced with a two-cushion one. In addition we had two enormous armchairs (one in my study, one in our bedroom) that pleaded to being of sentimental value as well as being comfortable, but no. They had to go. One could hardly open the door of the store cupboard to get at the cleaning gear and materials; the imbalance of its contents was marked by the presence of six (!) decanters, the symbols of the life of a wandering scholar who stayed long enough in various places to 'merit' some token of his departure.

In my parents' time it would have been the easiest thing in the world to have completed the furniture changeover in a week. The three large items would have been put in the weekly sale of chattels at the local auctioneers and we would grumble at the poor return we were given. If there were no takers, even at a price of zero, then at least we could have made a bonfire of them. Today, the time and money costs of disposal change all that. None of the items was fireproof and therefore, strictly speaking, they did not conform with legal requirements. They could be reupholstered and fireproofed but that would take time (find a fast-working upholsterer!) and would be expensive. I discovered by some roundabout way that one was entitled to have the furniture picked up by the local authority and consigned to the local dump. Somehow, some language difficulty with public officials intervened and I mistook the day of pick-up. However, it was agreed that the items could be picked up at a date convenient to the council tax payer – for a charge of £19.99. The council were told exactly where they would find the relevant items but their 'pickuppers' did not materialise – and I had already paid for them to do so! The items were by now congregated by the back door of our complex, and for a few days they seemed to look accusingly at me as I came and went. Eventually they disappeared. That was that, but then there was still the question of the chest of drawers that had survived disposal. I could not bring myself to add it to the list of *rejetés*. Its past life enchanted us. For many years it had served loyally as a prop in the Theatre Royal, York, in period plays before its antique-shop owner had eventually decided to dispose of it. It had cost us all of £14, and deserved an honourable retirement.

'Furnituritis' might offer a signal that the 'victim' had at least the intention of looking after him or herself, but independence connoted something much more specific. The earlier presentation of the argument (Chapter 8) at least implied that Margaret and I, now avowedly 'aged', hoped to fulfil the functions of a domestic bursar; that is to say we would hire help with cleaning, laundry and catering as we wanted them carried out and then, as it were, use these ingredients to produce a tolerable lifestyle – always, of course, monitored from time to time by visits from our children! With excellent outside help we managed right up to the moment when Margaret entered the hospice.

Relations were so well established with the helpers that it seemed natural to them – or so it appeared to me – that they should take me over, and their manager must have concurred. They have displayed such efficiency, kindness and tact, the last-named quality being apparent when I indicated that ever since I was a boy and later as a naval rating, I had known how to make beds and wash clothes; as the cook of our mess on the lower deck, I had even prepared a steam pudding that earned the approval of my messmates. No doubts were expressed at the veracity of these assertions. I was steered into undertaking a few tasks where I could do little harm if they were badly undertaken, such as loading and unloading the washing machine, helping in the drawing up of a shopping list and bagging the rubbish to go down the second-floor communal chute.

It is not easy to elude the benevolent dictatorship of such domestic experts. They have not gone quite so far as to present me with a *menu du jour*, although it would be ungracious not to receive gratefully the dishes that they insist on preparing to prevent one starving at supper time. They are not about in the evening, so I can slip out to the takeaway or ever-open supermarket and obtain that essential component of a balanced diet – a Dundee mutton pie.

DEFYING DECREPITUDE: A PERSONAL MEMOIR

Our combined efforts were bizarrely manifested in the discovery one day as I descended the Mound from the Old Town to Princes Street that I could only proceed any further with my hands in my pockets to prevent my trousers falling down. I made British Home Stores in time to avoid being arrested for indecent exposure, although I never feel secure with modern clip-on braces as recommended to me. Despite the helpers' ministrations and my good appetite, I had lost nearly a stone in six weeks.

I attribute their willingness to stay with me to their attachment to Margaret. I could not have managed without their recognition that I would not know how to begin an independent existence without their expert opinions on what domestic items I must keep and learn to use (under their watchful eye) and those that could be discarded. (How could a Victorian flat iron marked 'British Made' have survived a dozen removals?) Their collective female mind, plus that of Helen and her cousin Caroline, combined with their individual sensitivities, also brought to my attention what skill and understanding they had to exercise in recommending what should be the destination of Margaret's personal possessions. In a way they had an easy task, for Margaret never laid claim on the affections of anyone through the promise of a gift of inherited property.

'Routine' is not a description of the passage of time that academics with activist aspirations wish to have ascribed to them. Having been (fairly) labelled a professional dissenter, I plead guilty to the charge of striving to be different from the common practice of ritualising one's life – golf on Saturdays, kirk on Sundays, so to speak. I learnt my lesson during bereavement. I think I would have broken down completely if I had not come to welcome the signs and sounds or a daily routine – the 4am arrival of the milk van, the first 41 bus changing gear as it rounds the corner of our road, the clonk of the daily papers pushed through the letterbox by the paper boy (actually a girl at present, and always prompt), the arrival of the helper at 9am, the chime of our grandmother clock, which I enjoy so much that I stand ready with the winding up key well before it is scheduled to stop – and so on.

It was routine that governed my attempt to continue to defy decrepitude, and that entailed more regular visits to the surgery. Remember, we visited it together 15 years or so before, when it had already been explained that I had 'had a good innings'. Remember the route? It is exactly the same, but even with the help of my 'third leg' I find it quite an expedition negotiating the hilly path that takes me to the medical group, as it now describes itself. Sometimes I cheat and accept the offer of a lift.

Epilogue: the changing relationship between doctor and patient

In the long run, defying decrepitude looks more and more like an empty gesture. Any attempt to remain independent rests on the growing support sought for medical advice and attention. But even this sample may contain a preliminary lesson to be learnt about the collaboration that must develop between the givers and receivers of medical services designed to improve both the quality and the length of individual life. With major Western countries committed to improving the quality of life of all their citizens but faced with an ageing population, considerable attention must now be directed towards methods of reducing medical costs.

The attempt to remain independent as long as it is sensible to do so, as embodied in defying decrepitude, points towards an emphasis on seeking cost reduction through 'self-tracking'.[2] This piece of jargon has reached the stage of almost being overused, but it is useful shorthand for ways in which, to take medicine as an example, a patient can generate information on the progress of an illness, i.e. keep track on its development through the use of new technologies that monitor changes in the condition. The trick is to find ways in which patients themselves can act as monitors, thus releasing medical staff to concentrate on spreading the benefits of their diagnostic and therapeutic skills. Presumably prolonging the expectation of life carries with it a concomitant improvement in the health of the ageing, and therefore the prospect that self-tracking could be patients' contribution to looking after themselves. Of course, a considerable proportion of the old and sick suffer from illnesses that would preclude them from participation in tracking – possibly Parkinson's disease and dementia – but these are already marked down as illnesses for which cures may be found eventually.

The 'old banger' may become transformed, but in the end is denied transcendency. Scarcely a week goes by nowadays when I am not kindly reminded that my presence is required at this or that clinic. I have positively enjoyed cheerful badinage with the senior staff nurse wiring me up for my 'MOT' test to confirm that my pacemaker is in working order. At first it was once a year, then once every six months, but will shortly go down to every two months. And then, like the fitting of a new battery in a car of ancient vintage, the pacemaker has to be replaced. Simple job, I am told, with no need for more than a local anaesthetic; one can even be supplied with a screen to watch the whole process (not for me, I fear). But I am interested to know whether the fitter has to be a fully qualified surgeon or whether the process, eight years down the line, is now so simple that it is handed over to a trainee doctor or a fully experienced staff nurse.

Last summer I received preliminary notice of a 'summons' to the cardiology department of the Edinburgh Infirmary. It was clear in its non-specificity, and I could only assume that some sort of general check-up of my breathing system was planned. Had the moment come when some indication could be given of the amount of life left in the old banger? I had implicit faith in being given a straight answer, if I had the courage to recognise that defiance had reached its limit and I had to be the one who raised the question.

It was a summer of close scrutiny of the old banger. One thing was known: my pacemaker would have to be renewed or renovated. Nothing surprising there. Off to the Royal Infirmary I went, only suffering the long wait in the queue for the repair shop with no food allowed. I was so dazzled by the care and attention during the replacement that complaint of starvation seemed otiose. (The 'food' eventually turned up in the form of doorstep sandwiches reminiscent of those sold in British Rail buffets half a century ago.)

That was hardly enough to explain a loss of weight and appetite, and the diligent doctors in the practice decided that I was of an age when localised prostate cancer could be at work. Playing the old 'wag' again I produce this gruesome mixed metaphor: my prostate was my Achilles heel. It turns out that the only fearful part of the discovery process is being subjected to a scan. Treatment is initially simple: a needle in the buttocks every three months, and then? I am relieved to know the probable path of my decline, if not the speed of descent. A high hidden cost to the patient swiftly became evident: I lost entirely my taste for red wine. Do I really have to say goodbye to pinot noir and the recent discovery of the blessings of this noble grape as nurtured by the growers of the Italian Tyrol? Margaret would have understood the degree of deprivation that this would entail. But that is little enough to complain about.

Endnotes

[1] See A. Peacock and W. Pearson (2010), The Peacock versus the louse: one soldier's contribution to combating trench fever in the First World War, *Journal of the Royal College of Physicians of Edinburgh* **40**(3), 256–62. Available online at www.rcpe.ac.uk/journal/issue/journal_40_3/peacock.pdf.

2) See "The Dream of the Medical Tricorder", *The Economist Technology Quarterly* pp. 10-12, December 1, 2012.